CONGRATULATIONS . . . .

Welcome to the ranks of Cessna owners! Your Cessna has been designed and constructed to give you the most in performance, economy, and comfort. It is our desire that you will find flying it, either for business or pleasure, a pleasant and profitable experience.

This Owner's Manual has been prepared as a guide to help you get the most pleasure and utility from your Model 172/Skyhawk. It contains information about your Cessna's equipment, operating procedures, and performance; and suggestions for its servicing and care. We urge you to read it from cover to cover, and to refer to it frequently.

Our interest in your flying pleasure has not ceased with your purchase of a Cessna. World-wide, the Cessna Dealer Organization backed by the Cessna Service Department stands ready to serve you. The following services are offered by most Cessna Dealers:

THE CESSNA WARRANTY -- It is designed to provide you with the most comprehensive coverage possible:
   a. No exclusions
   b. Coverage includes parts and labor
   c. Available at Cessna Dealers world wide
   d. Best in the industry

Specific benefits and provisions of the warranty plus other important benefits for you are contained in your Customer Care Program book supplied with your aircraft. Warranty service is available to you at any authorized Cessna Dealer throughout the world upon presentation of your Customer Care Card which establishes your eligibility under the warranty.

FACTORY TRAINED PERSONNEL to provide you with courteous expert service.

FACTORY APPROVED SERVICE EQUIPMENT to provide you with the most efficient and accurate workmanship possible.

A STOCK OF GENUINE CESSNA SERVICE PARTS on hand when you need them.

THE LATEST AUTHORITATIVE INFORMATION FOR SERVICING CESSNA AIRPLANES, since Cessna Dealers have all of the Service Manuals and Parts Catalogs, kept current by Service Letters and Service News Letters, published by Cessna Aircraft Company.

We urge all Cessna owners to use the Cessna Dealer Organization to the fullest.

A current Cessna Dealer Directory accompanies your new airplane. The Directory is revised frequently, and a current copy can be obtained from your Cessna Dealer. Make your Directory one of your cross-country flight planning aids; a warm welcome awaits you at every Cessna Dealer.

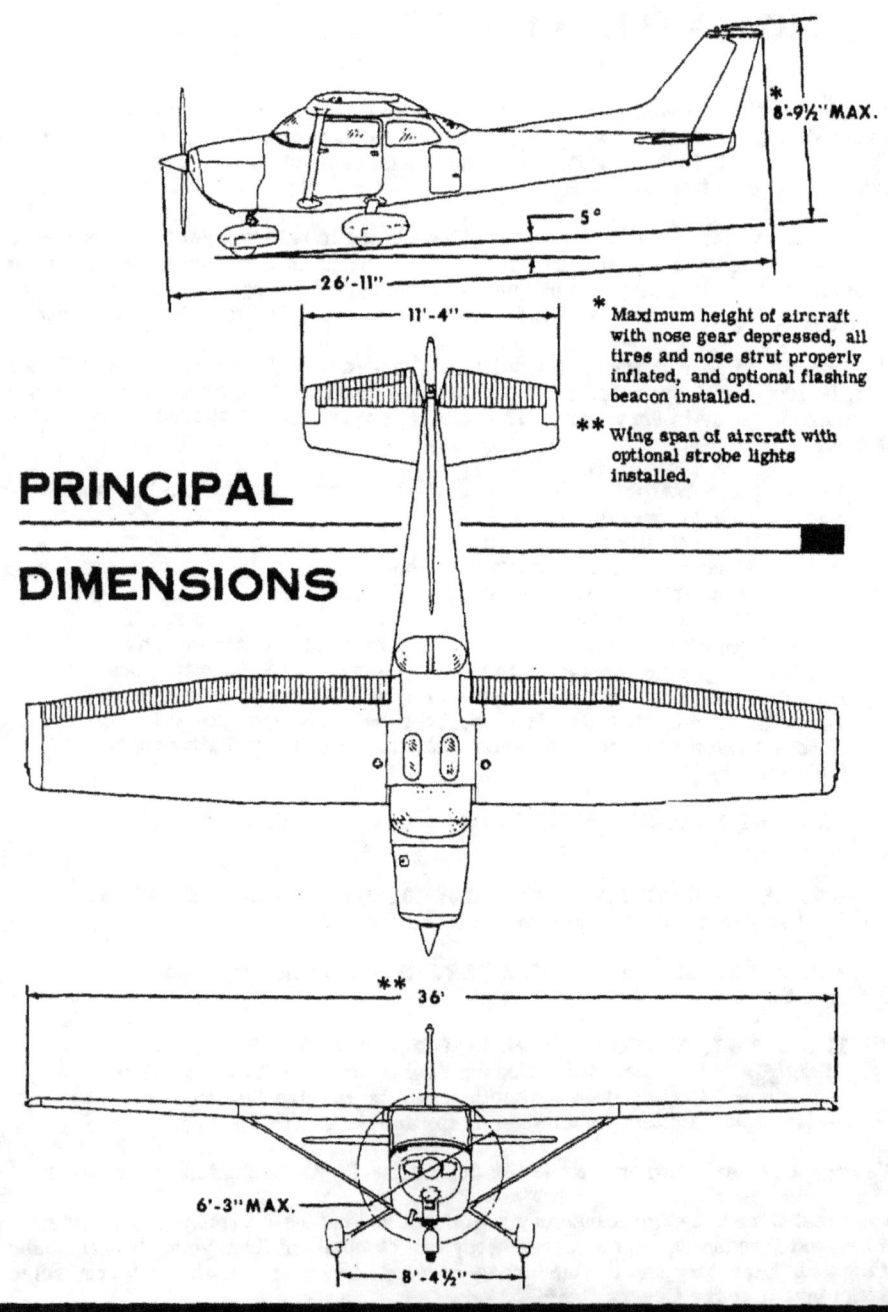

PRINCIPAL DIMENSIONS

* Maximum height of aircraft with nose gear depressed, all tires and nose strut properly inflated, and optional flashing beacon installed.

** Wing span of aircraft with optional strobe lights installed.

PERFORMANCE - SPECIFICATIONS

Skyhawk*

GROSS WEIGHT	2300 lbs
SPEED:	
Top Speed at Sea Level	144 mph
Cruise, 75% Power at 8000 ft	138 mph
RANGE:	
Cruise, 75% Power at 8000 ft	650 mi
38 Gallons, No Reserve	4.7 hrs
	138 mph
Cruise, 75% Power at 8000 ft	815 mi
48 Gallons, No Reserve	5.9 hrs
	138 mph
Maximum Range at 10,000 ft	700 mi
38 Gallons, No Reserve	6.0 hrs
	117 mph
Maximum Range at 10,000 ft	875 mi
48 Gallons, No Reserve	7.5 hrs
	117 mph
RATE OF CLIMB AT SEA LEVEL	645 fpm
SERVICE CEILING	13,100 ft
TAKE-OFF:	
Ground Run	865 ft
Total Distance Over 50-Foot Obstacle	1525 ft
LANDING:	
Ground Roll	520 ft
Total Distance Over 50-Foot Obstacle	1250 ft
STALL SPEED:	
Flaps Up, Power Off	57 mph
Flaps Down, Power Off	49 mph
BAGGAGE	120 lbs
WING LOADING: Pounds/Sq Foot	13.2
POWER LOADING: Pounds/HP	15.3
FUEL CAPACITY: Total	
Standard Tanks	42 gal.
Optional Long Range Tanks	52 gal.
OIL CAPACITY	8 qts
PROPELLER: Fixed Pitch, Diameter	75 inches
ENGINE:	
Lycoming Engine	O-320-E2D
150 rated HP at 2700 RPM	

	172	Skyhawk	Skyhawk II	F172 Skyhawk	F172 Skyhawk II
EMPTY WEIGHT: (Approximate)	1305 lbs	1350 lbs	1375 lbs	1335 lbs	1410 lbs
USEFUL LOAD: (Approximate)	995 lbs	950 lbs	925 lbs	965 lbs	890 lbs

NOTE: Speed performance data is shown for the Skyhawk which is one to four mph faster than a standard equipped Model 172 (without speed fairings), with the maximum difference occurring at top speed. There is a corresponding difference in range while all other performance figures are the same for the Model 172 as shown for the Skyhawk.

*This manual covers operation of the Model 172/Skyhawk which is certificated as Model 172M under FAA Type Certificate No. 3A12. The manual also covers operation of the Reims/Cessna F172 Skyhawk which is certificated as Model F172M under French Type Certificate No. 25 and FAA Type Certificate No. A4E.

Cessna Aircraft Company
Wichita, Kansas USA

TABLE OF CONTENTS

Page

SECTION I - OPERATING CHECKLIST 1-1

SECTION II - DESCRIPTION AND
             OPERATING DETAILS 2-1

SECTION III - EMERGENCY PROCEDURES 3-1

SECTION IV - OPERATING LIMITATIONS 4-1

SECTION V - CARE OF THE AIRPLANE 5-1

SECTION VI - OPERATIONAL DATA 6-1

SECTION VII - OPTIONAL SYSTEMS 7-1

ALPHABETICAL INDEX Index-1

This manual describes the operation and performance of the Model 172, the Skyhawk, and the Skyhawk II. Equipment described as "Optional" denotes that the subject equipment is optional on the Model 172. Much of this equipment is standard on the Skyhawk and Skyhawk II.

Section I

OPERATING CHECKLIST

One of the first steps in obtaining the utmost performance, service, and flying enjoyment from your Cessna is to familiarize yourself with your aircraft's equipment, systems, and controls. This can best be done by reviewing this equipment while sitting in the aircraft. Those items whose function and operation are not obvious are covered in Section II.

Section I lists, in Pilot's Checklist form, the steps necessary to operate your aircraft efficiently and safely. It is not a checklist in its true form as it is considerably longer, but it does cover briefly all of the points that you should know for a typical flight. A more convenient plastic enclosed checklist, stowed in the map compartment, is available for quickly checking that all important procedures have been performed. Since vigilance for other traffic is so important in crowded terminal areas, it is important that preoccupation with checklists be avoided in flight. Procedures should be carefully memorized and performed from memory. Then the checklist should be quickly scanned to ensure that nothing has been missed.

The flight and operational characteristics of your aircraft are normal in all respects. There are no "unconventional" characteristics or operations that need to be mastered. All controls respond in the normal way within the entire range of operation. All airspeeds mentioned in Sections I, II and III are indicated airspeeds. Corresponding calibrated airspeed may be obtained from the Airspeed Correction Table in Section VI.

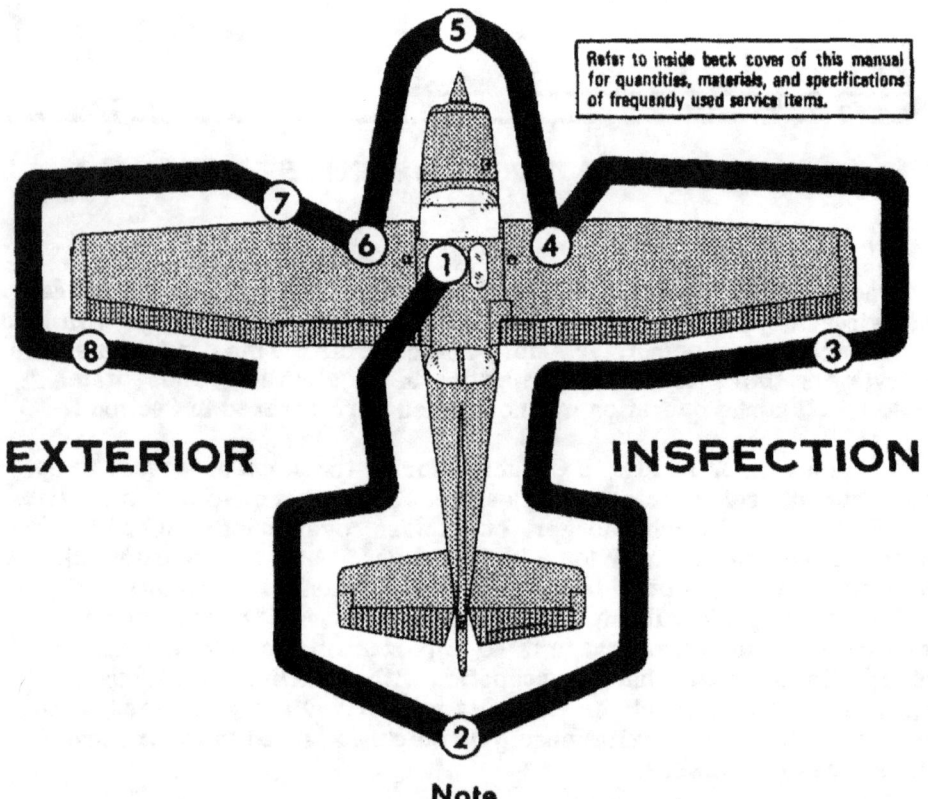

EXTERIOR INSPECTION

Note

Visually check aircraft for general condition during walk-around inspection. In cold weather, remove even small accumulations of frost, ice or snow from wing, tail and control surfaces. Also, make sure that control surfaces contain no internal accumulations of ice or debris. If night flight is planned, check operation of all lights, and make sure a flashlight is available.

① a. Remove control wheel lock.
    b. Check ignition switch OFF.
    c. Turn on master switch and check fuel quantity indicators; then turn off master switch.
    d. Check fuel selector valve handle on BOTH.
    e. Check baggage door for security. Lock with key if children are to occupy child's seat.

Figure

② a. Remove rudder gust lock, if installed.
b. Disconnect tail tie-down.
c. Check control surfaces for freedom of movement and security.

③ a. Check aileron for freedom of movement and security.

④ a. Disconnect wing tie-down.
b. Check main wheel tire for proper inflation.
c. Before first flight of the day and after each refueling, use sampler cup and drain small quantity of fuel from fuel tank sump quick-drain valve to check for water, sediment, and proper fuel grade.
d. Visually check fuel quantity; then check fuel filler cap secure.

⑤ a. Check oil level. Do not operate with less than six quarts. Fill to eight quarts for extended flights.
b. Before first flight of the day and after each refueling, pull out strainer drain knob for about four seconds to clear fuel strainer of possible water and sediment. Check strainer drain closed. If water is observed, the fuel system may contain additional water, and further draining of the system at the strainer, fuel tank sumps, and fuel selector valve drain plug will be necessary.
c. Check propeller and spinner for nicks and security.
d. Check landing light(s) for condition and cleanliness.
e. Check carburetor air filter for restrictions by dust or other foreign matter.
f. Check nose wheel strut and tire for proper inflation.
g. Disconnect tie-down rope.
h. Inspect flight instrument static source opening on side of fuselage for stoppage (left side only).

⑥ a. Check main wheel tire for proper inflation.
b. Before first flight of the day and after each refueling, use sampler cup and drain small quantity of fuel from fuel tank sump quick-drain valve to check for water, sediment, and proper fuel grade.
c. Visually check fuel quantity, then check fuel filler cap secure.

⑦ a. Remove pitot tube cover, if installed, and check pitot tube opening for stoppage.
b. Check fuel tank vent opening for stoppage.
c. Check stall warning vent opening for stoppage.
d. Disconnect wing tie-down.

⑧ a. Check aileron for freedom of movement and security.

1-1.

BEFORE STARTING ENGINE.

(1) Exterior Preflight -- COMPLETE.
(2) Seats, Belts, Shoulder Harnesses -- ADJUST and LOCK.
(3) Fuel Selector Valve -- BOTH.
(4) Radios, Autopilot, Electrical Equipment -- OFF.
(5) Brakes -- TEST and SET.

STARTING ENGINE.

(1) Mixture -- RICH.
(2) Carburetor Heat -- COLD.
(3) Master Switch -- ON.
(4) Prime -- AS REQUIRED (2 to 6 strokes; none if engine is warm).
(5) Throttle -- OPEN 1/8 INCH.
(6) Propeller Area -- CLEAR.
(7) Ignition Switch -- START (release when engine starts).
(8) Oil Pressure -- CHECK.

BEFORE TAKE-OFF.

(1) Parking Brake -- SET.
(2) Cabin Doors and Window -- CLOSED and LOCKED.
(3) Flight Controls -- FREE and CORRECT.
(4) Elevator Trim -- TAKE-OFF.
(5) Fuel Selector Valve -- BOTH.
(6) Mixture -- RICH (below 3000 ft.).
(7) Throttle -- 1700 RPM.
    a. Magnetos -- CHECK (RPM drop should not exceed 125 RPM on either magneto or 50 RPM differential between magnetos).
    b. Carburetor Heat -- CHECK (for RPM drop).
    c. Engine Instruments and Ammeter -- CHECK.
    d. Suction Gage -- CHECK.
(8) Flight Instruments and Radios -- SET.
(9) Optional Autopilot -- OFF.
(10) Throttle Friction Lock -- ADJUST.
(11) Wing Flaps -- UP.

TAKE-OFF.

NORMAL TAKE-OFF.

(1) Wing Flaps -- UP.
(2) Carburetor Heat -- COLD.
(3) Throttle -- FULL.
(4) Elevator Control -- LIFT NOSE WHEEL (at 60 MPH).
(5) Climb Speed -- 75 to 85 MPH.

MAXIMUM PERFORMANCE TAKE-OFF.

(1) Wing Flaps -- UP.
(2) Carburetor Heat -- COLD.
(3) Brakes -- APPLY.
(4) Throttle -- FULL.
(5) Brakes -- RELEASE.
(6) Airplane Attitude -- SLIGHTLY TAIL LOW.
(7) Climb Speed -- 68 MPH (until all obstacles are cleared).

ENROUTE CLIMB.

(1) Airspeed -- 80 to 90 MPH.

NOTE

If a maximum performance climb is necessary, use speeds shown in the Maximum Rate-Of-Climb Data chart in Section VI.

(2) Throttle -- FULL.
(3) Mixture -- FULL RICH (mixture may be leaned above 3000 feet).

CRUISE.

(1) Power -- 2200 to 2700 RPM (no more than 75%).
(2) Elevator Trim -- ADJUST.
(3) Mixture -- LEAN.

LET-DOWN.

   (1) Mixture -- RICH.
   (2) Power -- AS DESIRED.
   (3) Carburetor Heat -- AS REQUIRED (to prevent carburetor icing).

BEFORE LANDING.

   (1) Fuel Selector Valve -- BOTH.
   (2) Mixture -- RICH.
   (3) Carburetor Heat -- ON (apply full heat before closing throttle).
   (4) Airspeed -- 70 - 80 MPH (flaps UP).
   (5) Wing Flaps -- AS DESIRED.
   (6) Airspeed -- 65 - 75 MPH (flaps DOWN).

BALKED LANDING.

   (1) Throttle -- FULL.
   (2) Carburetor Heat -- COLD.
   (3) Wing Flaps -- 20°.
   (4) Airspeed -- 65 MPH.
   (5) Wing Flaps -- RETRACT (slowly).

NORMAL LANDING.

   (1) Touchdown -- MAIN WHEELS FIRST.
   (2) Landing Roll -- LOWER NOSE WHEEL GENTLY.
   (3) Braking -- MINIMUM REQUIRED.

AFTER LANDING.

   (1) Wing Flaps -- UP.
   (2) Carburetor Heat -- COLD.

SECURING AIRCRAFT.

(1) Parking Brake -- SET.
(2) Radios, Electrical Equipment, Autopilot -- OFF.
(3) Mixture -- IDLE CUT-OFF (pulled full out).
(4) Ignition Switch -- OFF.
(5) Master Switch -- OFF.
(6) Control Lock -- INSTALL.

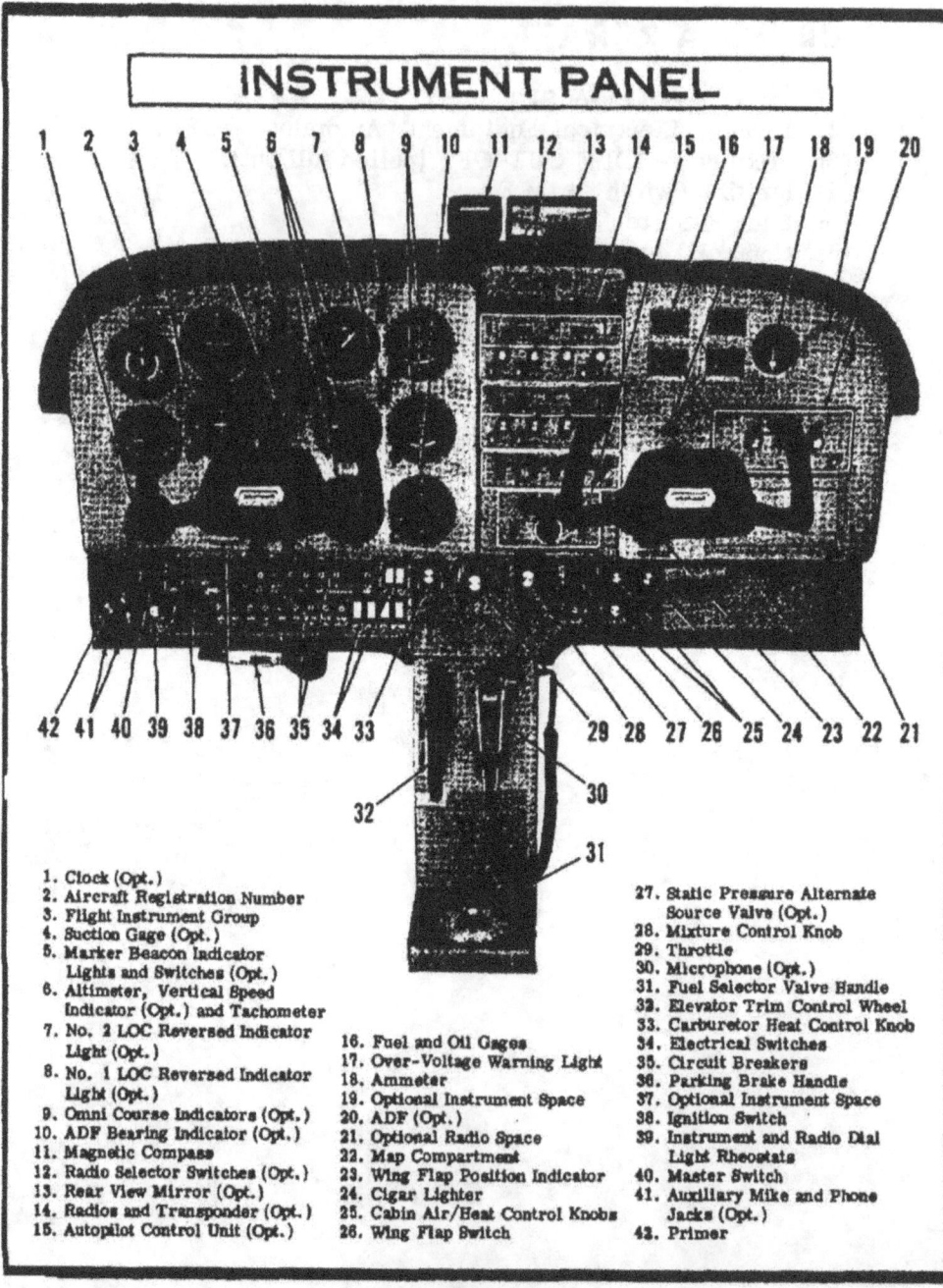

Figure 2-1.

1. Clock (Opt.)
2. Aircraft Registration Number
3. Flight Instrument Group
4. Suction Gage (Opt.)
5. Marker Beacon Indicator Lights and Switches (Opt.)
6. Altimeter, Vertical Speed Indicator (Opt.) and Tachometer
7. No. 2 LOC Reversed Indicator Light (Opt.)
8. No. 1 LOC Reversed Indicator Light (Opt.)
9. Omni Course Indicators (Opt.)
10. ADF Bearing Indicator (Opt.)
11. Magnetic Compass
12. Radio Selector Switches (Opt.)
13. Rear View Mirror (Opt.)
14. Radios and Transponder (Opt.)
15. Autopilot Control Unit (Opt.)
16. Fuel and Oil Gages
17. Over-Voltage Warning Light
18. Ammeter
19. Optional Instrument Space
20. ADF (Opt.)
21. Optional Radio Space
22. Map Compartment
23. Wing Flap Position Indicator
24. Cigar Lighter
25. Cabin Air/Heat Control Knobs
26. Wing Flap Switch
27. Static Pressure Alternate Source Valve (Opt.)
28. Mixture Control Knob
29. Throttle
30. Microphone (Opt.)
31. Fuel Selector Valve Handle
32. Elevator Trim Control Wheel
33. Carburetor Heat Control Knob
34. Electrical Switches
35. Circuit Breakers
36. Parking Brake Handle
37. Optional Instrument Space
38. Ignition Switch
39. Instrument and Radio Dial Light Rheostats
40. Master Switch
41. Auxiliary Mike and Phone Jacks (Opt.)
42. Primer

Section II

DESCRIPTION AND OPERATING DETAILS

The following paragraphs describe the systems and equipment whose function and operation is not obvious when sitting in the aircraft. This section also covers in somewhat greater detail some of the items listed in Checklist form in Section I that require further explanation.

FUEL SYSTEM.

Fuel is supplied to the engine from two tanks, one in each wing. With the fuel selector valve on BOTH, the total usable fuel for all flight conditions is 38 gallons for the standard tanks.

Fuel from each wing tank flows by gravity to a selector valve. Depending upon the setting of the selector valve, fuel from the left, right, or both tanks flows through a fuel strainer and carburetor to the engine induction system.

The fuel selector valve should be in the BOTH position for take-off, climb, landing, and maneuvers that involve prolonged slips or skids. Operation from either LEFT or RIGHT tank is reserved for cruising flight.

NOTE

With low fuel (1/8th tank or less), a prolonged steep descent (1500 feet or more) with partial power, full flaps, and 80 MPH or greater should be avoided due to the possibility of the fuel tank outlets being uncovered, causing temporary fuel starvation. If starvation occurs, leveling the nose should restore power within 20 seconds.

NOTE

When the fuel selector valve handle is in the BOTH position in cruising flight, unequal fuel flow from each

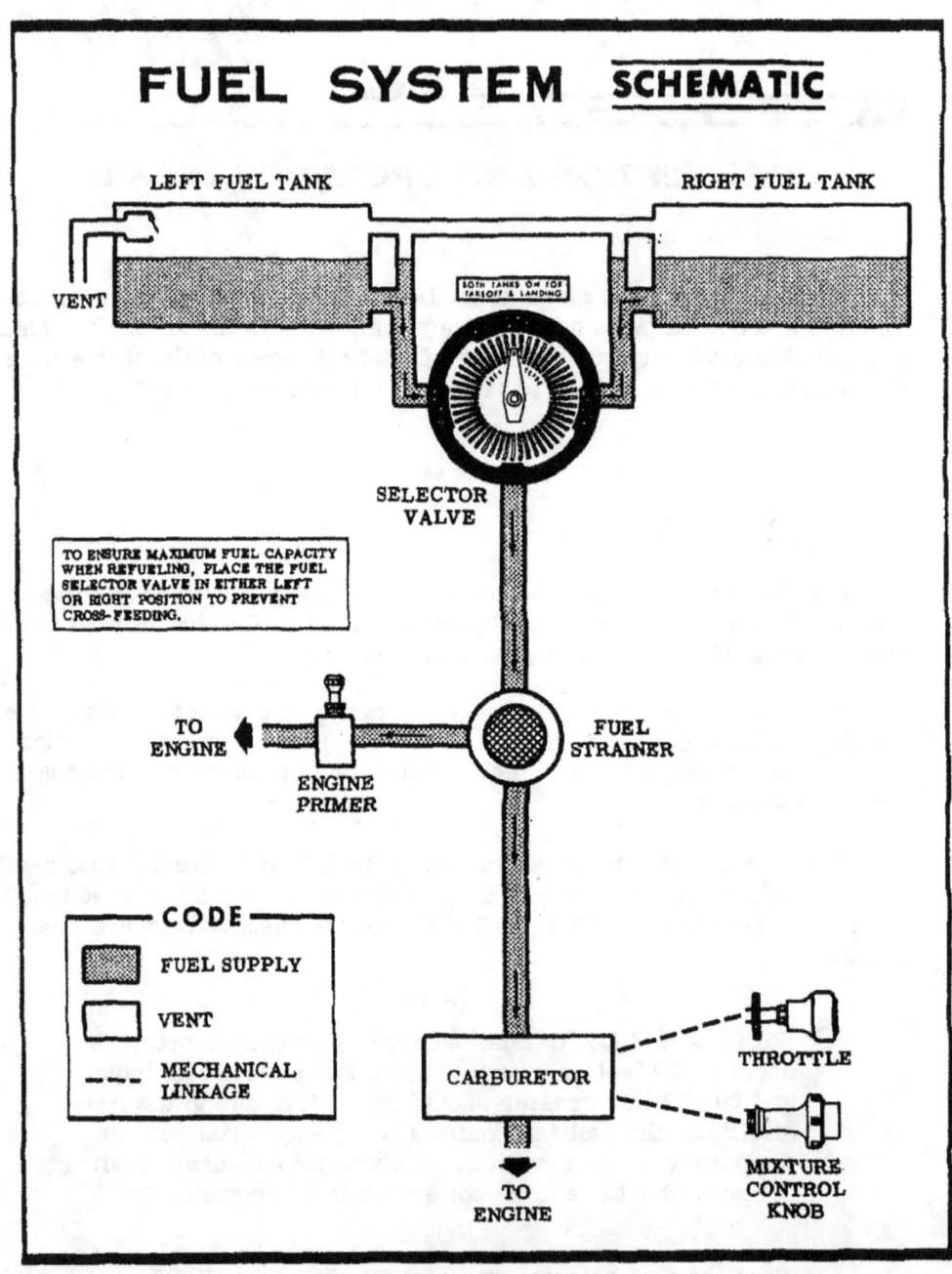

Figure 2-2.

tank may occur if the wings are not maintained exactly
level. Resulting wing heaviness can be alleviated
gradually by turning the selector valve handle to the
tank in the "heavy" wing.

NOTE

It is not practical to measure the time required to consume all of the fuel in one tank, and, after switching to the opposite tank, expect an equal duration from the remaining fuel. The airspace in both fuel tanks is interconnected by a vent line (figure 2-2) and, therefore, some sloshing of fuel between tanks can be expected when the tanks are nearly full and the wings are not level.

For fuel system servicing information, refer to Servicing Requirements on the inside back cover.

FUEL TANK SUMP QUICK-DRAIN VALVES.

Each fuel tank sump is equipped with a fuel quick-drain valve to facilitate draining and/or examination of fuel for contamination and grade. The valve extends through the lower surface of the wing just outboard of the cabin door. A sampler cup stored in the aircraft is used to examine the fuel. Insert the probe in the sampler cup into the center of the quick-drain valve and push. Fuel will drain from the tank sump into the sampler cup until pressure on the valve is released.

LONG RANGE FUEL TANKS.

Special wings with long range fuel tanks are available to replace the standard wings and fuel tanks for greater endurance and range. When these tanks are installed, the total usable fuel for all flight conditions is 48 gallons.

ELECTRICAL SYSTEM.

Electrical energy is supplied by a 14-volt, direct-current system powered by an engine-driven alternator (see figure 2-3). A 12-volt battery is located on the left-hand forward portion of the firewall. Power is supplied to all electrical circuits through a split bus bar, one side con-

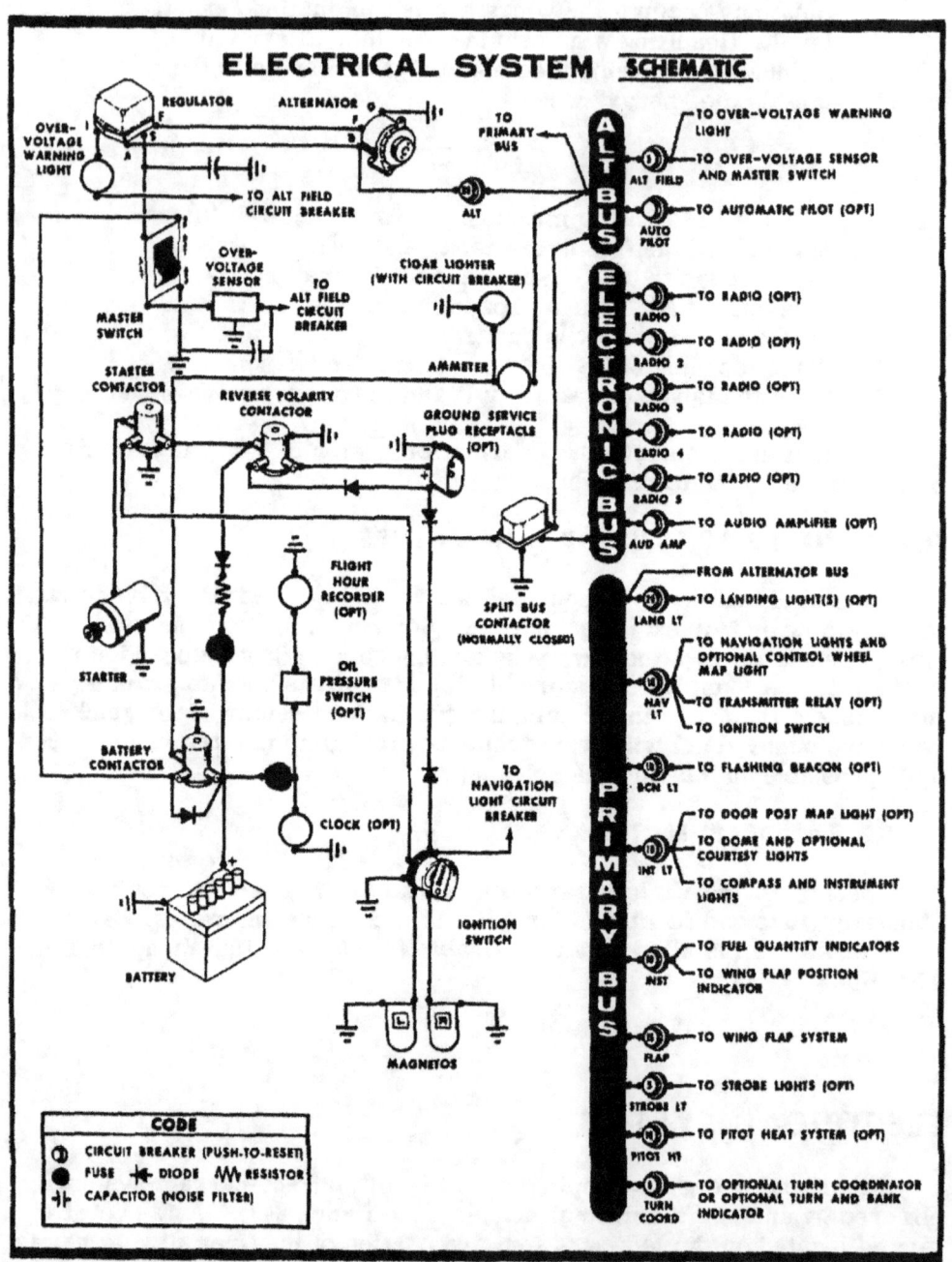

Figure 2-3.

taining electronic systems and the other side having general electrical systems. Both sides of the bus are on at all times except when either an external power source is connected or the ignition/starter switch is turned on; then a power contactor is automatically activated to open the circuit to the electronic bus. Isolating the electronic circuits in this manner prevents harmful transient voltages from damaging the transistors in the electronic equipment.

MASTER SWITCH.

The master switch is a split-rocker type switch labeled MASTER, and is ON in the up position and OFF in the down position. The right half of the switch, labeled BAT, controls all electrical power to the aircraft. The left half, labeled ALT controls the alternator.

Normally, both sides of the master switch should be used simultaneously; however, the BAT side of the switch could be turned ON separately to check equipment while on the ground. The ALT side of the switch, when placed in the OFF position, removes the alternator from the electrical system. With this switch in the OFF position, the entire electrical load is placed on the battery. Continued operation with the alternator switch in the OFF position will reduce battery power low enough to open the battery contactor, remove power from the alternator field, and prevent alternator restart.

AMMETER.

The ammeter indicates the flow of current, in amperes, from the alternator to the battery or from the battery to the aircraft electrical system. When the engine is operating and the master switch is ON, the ammeter indicates the charging rate applied to the battery. In the event the alternator is not functioning or the electrical load exceeds the output of the alternator, the ammeter indicates the discharge rate of the battery.

OVER-VOLTAGE SENSOR AND WARNING LIGHT.

The aircraft is equipped with an automatic over-voltage protection system consisting of an over-voltage sensor behind the instrument panel and a red warning light, labeled HIGH VOLTAGE, under the oil temperature and pressure gages.

In the event an over-voltage condition occurs, the over-voltage sensor automatically removes alternator field current and shuts down the alternator. The red warning light will then turn on, indicating to the pilot that the alternator is not operating and the aircraft battery is supplying all electrical power.

The over-voltage sensor may be reset by turning the master switch off and back on again. If the warning light does not illuminate, normal alternator charging has resumed; however, if the light does illuminate again, a malfunction has occurred, and the flight should be terminated as soon as practical.

The over-voltage warning light may be tested by momentarily turning off the ALT portion of the master switch and leaving the BAT portion turned on.

CIRCUIT BREAKERS AND FUSES.

The majority of electrical circuits in the aircraft are protected by "push-to-reset" circuit breakers mounted on the instrument panel. Exceptions to this are the optional clock and flight hour recorder circuits, and the battery contactor closing (external power) circuit which have fuses mounted adjacent to the battery. Also, the cigar lighter is protected by a manually reset type circuit breaker mounted directly on the back of the lighter behind the instrument panel.

When more than one radio is installed, the radio transmitter relay (which is a part of the radio installation) is protected by the navigation lights circuit breaker labeled NAV LT. It is important to remember that any malfunction in the navigation lights system which causes the circuit breaker to open will de-activate both the navigation lights and the transmitter relay. In this event, the navigation light switch should be turned off to isolate the circuit; then reset the circuit breaker to re-activate the transmitter relay and permit its usage. Do not turn on the navigation lights switch until the malfunction has been corrected.

LIGHTING EQUIPMENT.

EXTERIOR LIGHTING.

Conventional navigation lights are located on the wing tips and top of the rudder. Optional lighting includes a single landing light or dual landing/taxi lights in the cowl nose cap, a flashing beacon on the top of the vertical fin, a strobe light on each wing tip, and two courtesy lights, one under each wing, just outboard of the cabin door. The courtesy lights are controlled by the dome light switch located on the overhead console. All other exterior lights are controlled by rocker type switches located on the left switch and control panel. The switches are ON in the up position and OFF in the down position.

The flashing beacon should not be used when flying through clouds or overcast; the flashing light reflected from water droplets or particles in the atmosphere, particularly at night, can produce vertigo and loss of orientation.

The two high intensity strobe lights will enhance anti-collision protection. However, the lights should be turned off when taxiing in the vicinity of other aircraft, or during flight through clouds, fog or haze.

INTERIOR LIGHTING.

Illumination of the instrument panel is provided by red flood lighting in the forward portion of the overhead console. The magnetic compass and radio equipment have integral lighting. A dual rheostat control on the left switch and control panel operates these lights. The inner knob, labeled PANEL, operates the instrument panel and compass lighting. The outer knob, labeled RADIO, controls all radio lighting.

A cabin dome light is located in the overhead console, and is operated by a switch adjacent to the light. To turn the light on, move the switch to the right. This will also operate the optional courtesy lights.

An optional map light may be mounted on the bottom of the pilot's control wheel. The light illuminates the lower portion of the cabin, just forward of the pilot, and is helpful when checking maps and other flight data during night operations. To operate the light, first turn on the NAV LT switch, then adjust the map light's intensity with the disk type rheostat control located on the bottom of the control wheel.

A doorpost map light is also offered as optional equipment, and is located at the top of the left forward doorpost. The light contains both red and white bulbs, and may be positioned to illuminate any area desired by the pilot. A switch on the left forward doorpost is labeled RED, OFF, and WHITE. Placing the switch in the top position will provide a red light. In the bottom position, standard white lighting is provided. The center position is OFF.

WING FLAP SYSTEM.

The wing flaps are electrically operated by a flap motor located in the right wing. Flap position is controlled by a switch, labeled WING FLAPS on the lower center portion of the instrument panel. Flap position is shown by an indicator on the lower right portion of the instrument panel below the right control wheel position.

To extend the wing flaps, the flap switch must be depressed and held in the DOWN position until the desired degree of extension is reached. Releasing the switch allows it to return to the center off position. Normal full flap extension in flight will require approximately 9 seconds. After the flaps reach maximum extension or retraction, limit switches will automatically shut off the flap motor.

To retract the flaps, place the flap switch in the UP position. The switch will remain in the UP position without manual assistance due to an over-center design of the switch. Full flap retraction in flight requires approximately 7 seconds. More gradual flap retraction can be accomplished by intermittent operation of the flap switch to the UP position. After full retraction, the switch is normally returned to the center off position.

CABIN HEATING, VENTILATING AND DEFROSTING SYSTEM.

For cabin ventilation, pull the CABIN AIR knob out. To raise the air temperature, pull the CABIN HT knob out approximately 1/4" to 1/2" for a small amount of cabin heat. Additional heat is available by pulling the knob out farther; maximum heat is available with the CABIN HT knob pulled out and the CABIN AIR knob pushed full in. When no heat is desired in the cabin, the CABIN HT knob is pushed full in.

Front cabin heat and ventilating air is supplied by outlet holes spaced across a cabin manifold just forward of the pilot's and copilot's feet. Rear cabin heat and air is supplied by two ducts from the manifold, one extending down each side of the cabin to an outlet at the front door post at floor level. Windshield defrost air is also supplied by a duct leading from the cabin manifold. Two knobs control sliding valves in the defroster outlet and permit regulation of defroster airflow.

Separate adjustable ventilators supply additional air; one near each upper corner of the windshield supplies air for the pilot and copilot, and two optional ventilators in the rear cabin ceiling supply air to the rear seat passengers.

SHOULDER HARNESSES.

Shoulder harnesses are provided as standard equipment for the pilot and front seat passenger, and as optional equipment for the rear seat passengers. Seat belts are standard equipment for all passengers.

Each standard front seat harness is attached to a rear door post just above window line and is stowed behind a stowage sheath mounted above each cabin door. The optional rear seat shoulder harnesses are attached just behind the lower corners of the aft side windows. Each harness is stowed behind a stowage sheath located above the aft side window.

To use a standard front or optional rear seat shoulder harness, fasten and adjust the seat belt first. Remove the harness from the stowed position, and lengthen as required by pulling on the end of the harness and the narrow release strap. Snap the harness metal stud firmly into the retaining slot adjacent to the seat belt buckle. Then adjust to length by pulling down on the free end of the harness. A properly adjusted harness will permit the occupant to lean forward enough to sit completely erect but is tight enough to prevent excessive forward movement and contact with objects during sudden deceleration. Also, the pilot will want the freedom to reach all controls easily.

Releasing and removing the shoulder harness is accomplished by pulling upward on the narrow release strap and removing the harness stud from the slot in the seat belt buckle. In an emergency, the shoulder harness may be removed by releasing the seat belt first and pulling the harness over the head by pulling up on the release strap.

INTEGRATED SEAT BELT/SHOULDER HARNESSES WITH INERTIA REEL.

Optional integrated seat belt/shoulder harnesses with inertia reels are available for the pilot and front seat passenger. The seat belt/shoulder harnesses extend from inertia reels located in the cabin ceiling to attach points on the inboard side of the two front seats. A separate seat belt half and buckle is located on the outboard side of the seats. Inertia reels allow complete freedom of body movement. However, in the event of a sudden deceleration, they will lock up automatically to protect the occupants.

NOTE

The inertia reels are located for maximum shoulder harness comfort and safe retention of the seat occupants. This location requires that the shoulder harnesses cross near the top so that the right hand inertia reel serves the pilot and the left hand reel serves the front passenger. When fastening the harness, check to ensure the proper harness is being used.

To use the seat belt/shoulder harness, adjust the metal buckle half on the harness up far enough to allow it to be drawn across the lap of the occupant and be fastened into the outboard seat belt buckle. Adjust seat belt tension by pulling up on the shoulder harness. To remove the seat belt/shoulder harness, release the seat belt buckle and allow the inertia reel to draw the harness to the inboard side of the seat.

STARTING ENGINE.

During engine starting, open the throttle approximately 1/8 inch. In warm temperatures, one or two strokes of the primer should be sufficient. In cold weather, up to six strokes of the primer may be necessary. If the engine is warm, no priming will be required. In extremely cold temperatures, it may be necessary to continue priming while cranking the engine.

Weak intermittent firing followed by puffs of black smoke from the exhaust stack indicates overpriming or flooding. Excess fuel can be cleared from the combustion chambers by the following procedure: Set the mixture control full lean and the throttle full open; then crank the engine through several revolutions with the starter. Repeat the starting procedure without any additional priming.

If the engine is underprimed (most likely in cold weather with a cold engine) it will not fire at all, and additional priming will be necessary. As soon as the cylinders begin to fire, open the throttle slightly to keep it running.

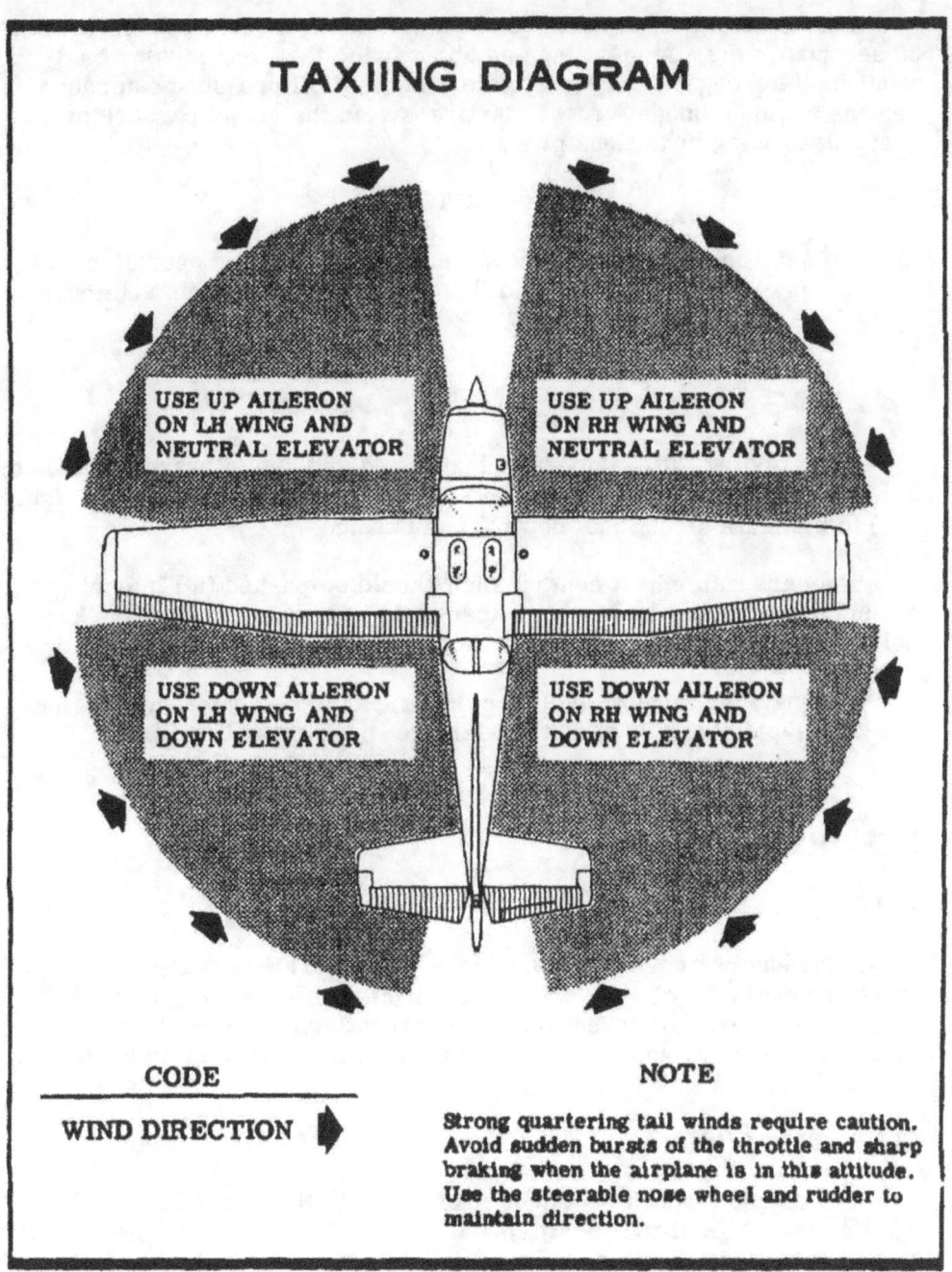

Figure 2-4.

After starting, if the oil gage does not begin to show pressure within 30 seconds in the summertime and about twice that long in very cold weather, stop engine and investigate. Lack of oil pressure can cause serious engine damage. After starting, avoid the use of carburetor heat unless icing conditions prevail.

NOTE

Additional details for cold weather starting and operation may be found under Cold Weather Operation in this section.

TAXIING.

When taxiing, it is important that speed and use of brakes be held to a minimum and that all controls be utilized (see Taxiing Diagram, figure 2-4) to maintain directional control and balance.

The carburetor heat control knob should be pushed full in during all ground operations unless heat is absolutely necessary. When the knob is pulled out to the heat position, air entering the engine is not filtered.

Taxiing over loose gravel or cinders should be done at low engine speed to avoid abrasion and stone damage to the propeller tips.

BEFORE TAKE-OFF.

WARM-UP.

If the engine accelerates smoothly, the aircraft is ready for take-off. Since the engine is closely cowled for efficient in-flight engine cooling, precautions should be taken to avoid overheating during prolonged engine operation on the ground. Also, long periods of idling may cause fouled spark plugs.

MAGNETO CHECK.

The magneto check should be made at 1700 RPM as follows. Move ignition switch first to R position and note RPM. Next move switch back to BOTH to clear the other set of plugs. Then move switch to the L position, note RPM and return the switch to the BOTH position. RPM drop should not exceed 125 RPM on either magneto or show greater than 50 RPM differential between magnetos. If there is a doubt concerning operation of the ignition system, RPM checks at higher engine speeds will usually confirm whether a deficiency exists.

An absence of RPM drop may be an indication of faulty grounding of one side of the ignition system or should be cause for suspicion that the magneto timing is set in advance of the setting specified.

ALTERNATOR CHECK.

Prior to flights where verification of proper alternator and voltage regulator operation is essential (such as night or instrument flights), a positive verification can be made by loading the electrical system momentarily (3 to 5 seconds) with the optional landing light (if so equipped), or by operating the wing flaps during the engine runup (1700 RPM). The ammeter will remain within a needle width of zero if the alternator and voltage regulator are operating properly.

TAKE-OFF.

POWER CHECK.

It is important to check full-throttle engine operation early in the take-off run. Any signs of rough engine operation or sluggish engine acceleration is good cause for discontinuing the take-off. If this occurs, you are justified in making a thorough full-throttle, static runup before another take-off is attempted. The engine should run smoothly and turn approximately 2270 to 2370 RPM with carburetor heat off and mixture full rich.

NOTE

Carburetor heat should not be used during take-off unless it is absolutely necessary for obtaining smooth engine acceleration.

Full-throttle runups over loose gravel are especially harmful to propeller tips. When take-offs must be made over a gravel surface, it is very important that the throttle be advanced slowly. This allows the airplane to start rolling before high RPM is developed, and the gravel will be blown back of the propeller rather than pulled into it. When unavoidable small dents appear in the propeller blades, they should be immediately corrected as described in Section V under propeller care.

Prior to take-off from fields above 3000 feet elevation, the mixture should be leaned to give maximum RPM in a full-throttle, static runup.

After full throttle is applied, adjust the throttle friction lock clockwise to prevent the throttle from creeping back from a maximum power position. Similar friction lock adjustments should be made as required in other flight conditions to maintain a fixed throttle setting.

WING FLAP SETTINGS.

Normal and obstacle clearance take-offs are performed with wing flaps up. The use of 10° flaps will shorten the ground run approximately 10%, but this advantage is lost in the climb to a 50-foot obstacle. Therefore, the use of 10° flaps is reserved for minimum ground runs or for take-off from soft or rough fields. If 10° of flaps are used for minimum ground runs, it is preferable to leave them extended rather than retract them in the climb to the obstacle. In this case, use an obstacle clearance speed of 65 MPH. As soon as the obstacle is cleared, the flaps may be retracted as the aircraft accelerates to the normal flaps-up climb speed of 80 to 90 MPH.

During a high altitude take-off in hot weather where climb would be marginal with 10° flaps, it is recommended that the flaps not be used for take-off. Flap settings greater than 10° are not recommended at any time for take-off.

PERFORMANCE CHARTS.

Consult the Take-Off Data chart in Section VI for take-off distances under various gross weight, altitude, headwind, temperature, and runway surface conditions.

CROSSWIND TAKE-OFFS.

Take-offs into strong crosswinds normally are performed with the minimum flap setting necessary for the field length to minimize the drift angle immediately after take-off. The aircraft is accelerated to a speed slightly higher than normal, then pulled off abruptly to prevent possible settling back to the runway while drifting. When clear of the ground, make a coordinated turn into the wind to correct for drift.

ENROUTE CLIMB.

CLIMB DATA.

For detailed data, refer to the Maximum Rate-Of-Climb Data chart in Section VI.

CLIMB SPEEDS.

Normal climbs are performed at 80 to 90 MPH with flaps up and full throttle for best engine cooling. The mixture should be full rich below 3000 feet and may be leaned above 3000 feet for smoother engine operation or to obtain maximum RPM for maximum performance climb. The maximum rate-of-climb speeds range from 91 MPH at sea level to 80 MPH at 10,000 feet. If an enroute obstruction dictates the use of a steep climb angle, climb at 75 MPH with flaps retracted.

NOTE

Steep climbs at low speeds should be of short duration to improve engine cooling.

CRUISE.

Normal cruising is done at power settings up to 75% power. The engine RPM and corresponding fuel consumption for various altitudes can be determined by using your Cessna Power Computer or the Operational Data in Section VI.

The Operational Data in Section VI shows the increased range and improved fuel economy that is obtainable when operating at lower power settings and higher altitudes. The use of lower power settings and the selection of cruise altitude on the basis of the most favorable wind conditions are significant factors that should be considered on every trip to reduce fuel consumption.

The Cruise Performance table on the following page shows the true airspeed and miles per gallon during cruise for various altitudes and percent powers. This table should be used as a guide, along with the available winds aloft information, to determine the most favorable altitude and power setting for a given trip.

CRUISE PERFORMANCE
SKYHAWK

ALTITUDE	75% POWER		65% POWER		55% POWER	
	TAS	MPG	TAS	MPG	TAS	MPG
Sea Level	128	15.4	121	16.8	111	17.3
4000 Feet	133	16.0	125	17.4	114	17.8
8000 Feet	138	16.6	129	17.9	117	18.3

Standard Conditions   Zero Wind

To achieve the lean mixture fuel consumption figures shown in Section VI, the mixture should be leaned as follows:

(1) Pull the mixture control out until engine RPM peaks and begins to fall off.
(2) Enrichen slightly back to peak RPM.

For best fuel economy at 75% power or less, operate at the leanest mixture that results in smooth engine operation or at 50 RPM on the lean side of the peak RPM, whichever occurs first. This will result in approximately 5% greater range than shown in this manual.

Carburetor ice, as evidenced by an unexplained drop in RPM, can be removed by application of full carburetor heat. Upon regaining the original RPM (with heat off), use the minimum amount of heat (by trial and error) to prevent ice from forming. Since the heated air causes a richer mixture, readjust the mixture setting when carburetor heat is to be used continuously in cruise flight.

The use of full carburetor heat is recommended during flight in heavy rain to avoid the possibility of engine stoppage due to excessive water ingestion or carburetor ice. The mixture setting should be readjusted for smoothest operation.

In extremely heavy rain, the use of partial carburetor heat (control approximately 2/3 out), and part throttle (closed at least one inch), may be necessary to retain adequate power. Power changes should be made cautiously followed by prompt adjustment of the mixture for smoothest operation.

STALLS.

The stall characteristics are conventional and aural warning is provided by a stall warning horn which sounds between 5 and 10 MPH above the stall in all configurations.

Power-off stall speeds at maximum gross weight and aft c. g. position are presented on page 6-2 as calibrated airspeeds since indicated airspeeds are unreliable near the stall.

SPINS.

Intentional spins are approved in this aircraft in the Utility Category only. Although this aircraft is inherently resistant to spins, the following techniques may be used to perform intentional spins for training or practice. To obtain a clean entry, decelerate the aircraft at a faster rate than is used for stalls. Then, just as the stall occurs, apply full up elevator, full rudder in the desired spin direction, and momentarily use full engine power. As the aircraft begins to spin, reduce the power to idle and maintain full pro-spin elevator and rudder deflections. The application of ailerons in the direction of the desired spin may also help obtain a clean entry.

During extended spins of two to three turns or more, the spin will tend to change into a spiral, particularly to the right. This will be accompanied by an increase in airspeed and gravity loads on the aircraft. If this occurs, recovery should be accomplished quickly by leveling the wings and recovering from the resulting dive.

To recover from an intentional or inadvertent spin, use the following procedure:

(1) Retard throttle to idle position.
(2) Apply full rudder opposite to the direction of rotation.
(3) After one-fourth turn, move the control wheel forward of neutral in a brisk motion.

(4) As the rotation stops, neutralize the rudder, and make a smooth recovery from the resulting dive.

Intentional spins with flaps extended are prohibited.

LANDINGS.

Normal landings are made power-off with any flap setting desired. Steep slips should be avoided with flap settings greater than 20° due to a slight tendency for the elevator to oscillate under certain combinations of airspeed, sideslip angle, and center of gravity loadings.

NOTE

Carburetor heat should be applied prior to any significant reduction or closing of the throttle.

NORMAL LANDING.

Landings should be made on the main wheels first to reduce the landing speed and subsequent need for braking in the landing roll. The nose wheel is lowered to the runway gently after the speed has diminshed to avoid unnecessary nose gear loads. This procedure is especially important in rough or soft field landings.

SHORT FIELD LANDING.

For short field landings, make a power-off approach at approximately 70 MPH indicated airspeed with 40° of flaps. Touchdown should be made on the main wheels first. Immediately after touchdown, lower the nose gear to the ground and apply heavy braking as required. For maximum brake effectiveness after all three wheels are on the ground, retract the flaps, hold full nose up elevator and apply maximum possible brake pressure without sliding the tires.

CROSSWIND LANDING.

When landing in a strong crosswind, use the minimum flap setting required for the field length. If flap settings greater than 20° are used in sideslips with full rudder deflection, some elevator oscillation may be felt at normal approach speeds. However, this does not affect control of the aircraft. Although the crab or combination method of drift correction may be used, the wing-low method gives the best control. After touchdown, hold a straight course with the steerable nose wheel and occasional braking if necessary.

The maximum allowable crosswind velocity is dependent upon pilot capability rather than aircraft limitations. With average pilot technique, direct crosswinds of 15 knots can be handled with safety.

BALKED LANDING.

In a balked landing (go-around) climb, reduce the wing flap setting to 20° immediately after full power is applied. If the flaps were extended to 40°, the reduction to 20° may be approximated by placing the flap switch in the UP position for two seconds and then returning the switch to neutral. If obstacles must be cleared during the go-around climb, leave the wing flaps in the 10° to 20° range and maintain a climb speed of 65 to 75 MPH until the obstacles are cleared. Above 3000 feet, lean the mixture to obtain maximum RPM. After clearing any obstacles, the flaps may be retracted as the aircraft accelerates to the normal flaps-up climb speed of 80 to 90 MPH.

COLD WEATHER OPERATION.

STARTING.

Prior to starting on a cold morning, it is advisable to pull the propeller through several times by hand to "break loose" or "limber" the oil, thus conserving battery energy.

NOTE

When pulling the propeller through by hand, treat it as if the ignition switch is turned on. A loose or broken ground wire on either magneto could cause the engine to fire.

In extremely cold (0°F and lower) weather, the use of an external preheater and an external power source are recommended whenever possible to obtain positive starting and to reduce wear and abuse to the engine and electrical system. Pre-heat will thaw the oil trapped in the oil cooler, which probably will be congealed prior to starting in extremely cold temperatures. When using an external power source, the position of the master switch is important. Refer to Section VII under Ground Service Plug Receptacle for operating details.

Cold weather starting procedures are as follows:

<u>With Preheat:</u>

(1) With ignition switch OFF and throttle closed, prime the engine four to eight strokes as the propeller is being turned over by hand.

NOTE

Use heavy strokes of primer for best atomization of fuel. After priming, push primer all the way in and turn to locked position to avoid possibility of engine drawing fuel through the primer.

(2) Propeller Area -- CLEAR.
(3) Master Switch -- ON.
(4) Mixture -- FULL RICH.
(5) Throttle -- OPEN 1/8".
(6) Ignition Switch -- START.
(7) Release ignition switch to BOTH when engine starts.
(8) Oil Pressure -- CHECK.

<u>Without Preheat:</u>

(1) Prime the engine six to ten strokes while the propeller is being turned by hand with throttle closed. Leave primer charged and ready for stroke.
(2) Propeller Area -- CLEAR.
(3) Master Switch -- ON.
(4) Mixture -- FULL RICH.
(5) Ignition Switch -- START.
(6) Pump throttle rapidly to full open twice. Return to 1/8" open position.
(7) Release ignition switch to BOTH when engine starts.
(8) Continue to prime engine until it is running smoothly, or alternately pump throttle rapidly over first 1/4 to total travel.
(9) Oil Pressure -- CHECK.
(10) Pull carburetor heat knob full on after engine has started. Leave on until engine is running smoothly.
(11) Lock Primer.

NOTE

If the engine does not start during the first few attempts, or if the engine firing diminishes in strength, it is probable that the spark plugs have been frosted over. Preheat must be used before another start is attempted.

IMPORTANT

Pumping the throttle may cause raw fuel to accumulate in the intake air duct, creating a fire hazard in the event of a backfire. If this occurs, maintain a cranking action to suck flames into the engine. An outside attendant with a fire extinguisher is advised for cold starts without preheat.

During cold weather operations, no indication will be apparent on the oil temperature gage prior to take-off if outside air temperatures are very cold. After a suitable warm-up period (2 to 5 minutes at 1000 RPM), accelerate the engine several times to higher engine RPM. If the engine accelerates smoothly and the oil pressure remains normal and steady, the aircraft is ready for take-off.

FLIGHT OPERATIONS.

Take-off is made normally with carburetor heat off. Avoid excessive leaning in cruise.

Carburetor heat may be used to overcome any occasional engine roughness due to ice.

When operating in sub-zero temperature, avoid using partial carburetor heat. Partial heat may increase the carburetor air temperature to the 32° to 70°F range, where icing is critical under certain atmospheric conditions.

Refer to Section VII for cold weather equipment.

HOT WEATHER OPERATION.

Refer to the general warm temperature starting information under Starting Engine in this section. Avoid prolonged engine operation on the ground.

NOISE ABATEMENT.

Increased emphasis on improving the quality of our environment requires renewed effort on the part of all pilots to minimize the effect of aircraft noise on the public.

We, as pilots, can demonstrate our concern for environmental improvement, by application of the following suggested procedures, and thereby tend to build public support for aviation:

(1) Pilots operating aircraft under VFR over outdoor assemblies of persons, recreational and park areas, and other noise-sensitive areas should make every effort to fly not less than 2,000 feet above the surface, weather permitting, even though flight at a lower level may be consistent with the provisions of government regulations.
(2) During departure from or approach to an airport, climb after take-off and descent for landing should be made so as to avoid prolonged flight at low altitude near noise-sensitive areas.

NOTE

The above recommended procedures do not apply where they would conflict with Air Traffic Control clearances or instructions, or where, in the pilot's judgement, an altitude of less than 2,000 feet is necessary for him to adequately exercise his duty to see and avoid other aircraft.

Section III

EMERGENCY PROCEDURES

Emergencies caused by aircraft or engine malfunctions are extremely rare if proper pre-flight inspections and maintenance are practiced. Enroute weather emergencies can be minimized or eliminated by careful flight planning and good judgement when unexpected weather is encountered. However, should an emergency arise the basic guidelines described in this section should be considered and applied as necessary to correct the problem.

ENGINE FAILURE.

ENGINE FAILURE AFTER TAKE-OFF.

Prompt lowering of the nose to maintain airspeed and establish a glide attitude is the first response to an engine failure after take-off. In most cases, the landing should be planned straight ahead with only small changes in direction to avoid obstructions. Altitude and airspeed are seldom sufficient to execute a 180° gliding turn necessary to return to the runway. The following procedures assume that adequate time exists to secure the fuel and ignition systems prior to touchdown.

(1) Airspeed -- 75 MPH (flaps UP).
               70 MPH (flaps DOWN).
(2) Mixture -- IDLE CUT-OFF.
(3) Fuel Selector Valve -- OFF.
(4) Ignition Switch -- OFF.
(5) Wing Flaps -- AS REQUIRED (40° recommended).
(6) Master Switch -- OFF.

ENGINE FAILURE DURING FLIGHT.

While gliding toward a suitable landing area, an effort should be made to identify the cause of the failure. If time permits, and an engine restart is feasible, proceed as follows:

    (1) Airspeed -- 80 MPH.
    (2) Carburetor Heat -- ON.
    (3) Fuel Selector Valve -- BOTH.
    (4) Mixture -- RICH.
    (5) Ignition Switch -- BOTH (or START if propeller is not windmilling)
    (6) Primer -- IN and LOCKED.

If the engine cannot be restarted, a forced landing without power must be executed. A recommended procedure for this is given in the following paragraph.

FORCED LANDINGS.

EMERGENCY LANDING WITHOUT ENGINE POWER.

If all attempts to restart the engine fail and a forced landing is imminent, select a suitable field and prepare for the landing as follows:

    (1) Airspeed -- 75 MPH (flaps UP).
                      70 MPH (flaps DOWN).
    (2) Mixture -- IDLE CUT-OFF.
    (3) Fuel Selector Valve -- OFF.
    (4) Ignition Switch -- OFF.
    (5) Wing Flaps -- AS REQUIRED (40° recommended).
    (6) Master Switch -- OFF.
    (7) Doors -- UNLATCH PRIOR TO TOUCHDOWN.
    (8) Touchdown -- SLIGHTLY TAIL LOW.
    (9) Brakes -- APPLY HEAVILY.

PRECAUTIONARY LANDING WITH ENGINE POWER.

Before attempting an "off airport" landing, one should drag the landing area at a safe but low altitude to inspect the terrain for obstructions and surface conditions, proceeding as follows:

    (1) Drag over selected field with flaps 20° and 70 MPH airspeed, noting the preferred area for touchdown for the next landing approach. Then retract flaps upon reaching a safe altitude and airspeed.
    (2) Radio, Electrical Switches -- OFF.
    (3) Wing Flaps -- 40° (on final approach).

(4) Airspeed -- 70 MPH.
(5) Master Switch -- OFF.
(6) Doors -- UNLATCH PRIOR TO TOUCHDOWN.
(7) Touchdown -- SLIGHTLY TAIL LOW.
(8) Ignition Switch -- OFF.
(9) Brakes -- APPLY HEAVILY.

DITCHING.

Prepare for ditching by securing or jettisoning heavy objects located in the baggage area, and collect folded coats or cushions for protection of occupant's face at touchdown. Transmit Mayday message on 121.5 MHz. giving location and intentions.

(1) Plan approach into wind if winds are high and seas are heavy. With heavy swells and light wind, land parallel to swells.
(2) Approach with flaps 40° and sufficient power for a 300 ft./min. rate of descent at 70 MPH
(3) Unlatch the cabin doors.
(4) Maintain a continuous descent until touchdown in level attitude. Avoid a landing flare because of difficulty in judging aircraft height over a water surface.
(5) Place folded coat or cushion in front of face at time of touchdown.
(6) Evacuate aircraft through cabin doors. If necessary, open window to flood cabin compartment for equalizing pressure so that door can be opened.
(7) Inflate life vests and raft (if available) after evacuation of cabin. The aircraft cannot be depended on for flotation for more than a few minutes.

FIRES.

ENGINE FIRE DURING START ON GROUND.

Improper starting procedures during a difficult cold weather start can cause a backfire which could ignite fuel that has accumulated in the intake duct. In this event, proceed as follows:

(1) Continue cranking in an attempt to get a start which would suck the flames and accumulated fuel through the carburetor and into the engine.
(2) If the start is successful, run the engine at 1700 RPM for a few

minutes before shutting it down to inspect the damage.
(3) If engine start is unsuccessful, continue cranking for two or three minutes with throttle full open while ground attendants obtain fire extinguishers.
(4) When ready to extinguish fire, discontinue cranking and turn off master switch, ignition switch, and fuel selector valve.
(5) Smother flames with fire extinguisher, seat cushion, wool blanket, or loose dirt. If practical, try to remove carburetor air filter if it is ablaze.
(6) Make a thorough inspection of fire damage, and repair or replace damaged components before conducting another flight.

ENGINE FIRE IN FLIGHT.

Although engine fires are extremely rare in flight, the following steps should be taken if one is encountered:

(1) Mixture -- IDLE CUT-OFF.
(2) Fuel Selector Valve -- OFF.
(3) Master Switch -- OFF.
(4) Cabin Heat and Air -- OFF (except overhead vents).
(5) Airspeed -- 120 MPH. If fire is not extinguished, increase glide speed to find an airspeed which will provide an incombustible mixture.

Execute a forced landing as outlined in preceding paragraphs.

ELECTRICAL FIRE IN FLIGHT.

The initial indication of an electrical fire is usually the odor of burning insulation. The following procedure should then be used:

(1) Master Switch -- OFF.
(2) All Radio/Electrical Switches -- OFF.
(3) Vents/Cabin Air/Heat -- CLOSED.
(4) Fire Extinguisher -- ACTIVATE (if available).

If fire appears out and electrical power is necessary for continuance of flight:

(5) Master Switch -- ON.
(6) Circuit Breakers -- CHECK for faulty circuit, do not reset.
(7) Radio/Electrical Switches -- ON one at a time, with delay after each until short circuit is localized.

(8) Vents/Cabin Air/Heat -- OPEN when it is ascertained that fire is completely extinguished.

DISORIENTATION IN CLOUDS.

In the event of a vacuum system failure during flight in marginal weather, the directional gyro and gyro horizon will be disabled, and the pilot will have to rely on the turn coordinator or the turn and bank indicator if he inadvertently flies into clouds. The following instructions assume that only the electrically-powered turn coordinator or the turn and bank indicator is operative, and that the pilot is not completely proficient in partial panel instrument flying.

EXECUTING A 180° TURN IN CLOUDS.

Upon entering the clouds, an immediate plan should be made to turn back as follows:

(1) Note the time of the minute hand and observe the position of the sweep second hand on the clock.
(2) When the sweep second hand indicates the nearest half-minute, initiate a standard rate left turn, holding the turn coordinator symbolic aircraft wing opposite the lower left index mark for 60 seconds. Then roll back to level flight by leveling the miniature aircraft.
(3) Check accuracy of the turn by observing the compass heading which should be the reciprocal of the original heading.
(4) If necessary, adjust heading primarily with skidding motions rather than rolling motions so that the compass will read more accurately.
(5) Maintain altitude and airspeed by cautious application of elevator control. Avoid overcontrolling by keeping the hands off the control wheel and steering only with rudder.

EMERGENCY LET-DOWNS THROUGH CLOUDS.

If possible, obtain radio clearance for an emergency descent through clouds. To guard against a spiral dive, choose an easterly or westerly heading to minimize compass card swings due to changing bank angles. In addition, keep hands off the control wheel and steer a straight course with rudder control by monitoring the turn coordinator. Occasionally check the compass heading and make minor corrections to hold an approximate course. Before descending into the clouds, set up a stabilized let-down condition as follows:

    (1) Apply full rich mixture.
    (2) Use full carburetor heat.
    (3) Reduce power to set up a 500 to 800 ft./min. rate of descent.
    (4) Adjust the elevator trim tab for a stabilized descent at 80 to 90 MPH.
    (5) Keep hands off the control wheel.
    (6) Monitor turn coordinator and make corrections by rudder alone.
    (7) Check trend of compass card movement and make cautious corrections with rudder to stop the turn.
    (8) Upon breaking out of clouds, resume normal cruising flight.

RECOVERY FROM A SPIRAL DIVE.

If a spiral is encountered, proceed as follows:

    (1) Close the throttle.
    (2) Stop the turn by using coordinated aileron and rudder control to align the symbolic aircraft in the turn coordinator with the horizon reference line.
    (3) Cautiously apply elevator back pressure to slowly reduce the indicated airspeed to 90 MPH.
    (4) Adjust the elevator trim control to maintain a 90 MPH glide.
    (5) Keep hands off the control wheel, using rudder control to hold a straight heading.
    (6) Apply carburetor heat.
    (7) Clear engine occasionally, but avoid using enough power to disturb the trimmed glide.
    (8) Upon breaking out of clouds, apply normal cruising power and resume flight.

FLIGHT IN ICING CONDITIONS.

Although flying in known icing conditions is prohibited, an unexpected icing encounter should be handled as follows:

    (1) Turn pitot heat switch ON (if installed).
    (2) Turn back or change altitude to obtain an outside air temperature that is less conducive to icing.
    (3) Pull cabin heat control full out and open defroster outlet to obtain maximum windshield defroster airflow. Adjust cabin air control to

get maximum defroster heat and airflow.
(4) Open the throttle to increase engine speed and minimize ice build-up on propeller blades.
(5) Watch for signs of carburetor air filter ice and apply carburetor heat as required. An unexplained loss in engine speed could be caused by carburetor ice or air intake filter ice. Lean the mixture for maximum RPM if carburetor heat is used continuously.
(6) Plan a landing at the nearest airport. With an extremely rapid ice build-up, select a suitable "off airport" landing site.
(7) With an ice accumulation of 1/4 inch or more on the wing leading edges, be prepared for significantly higher stall speed.
(8) Leave wing flaps retracted. With a severe ice build-up on the horizontal tail, the change in wing wake airflow direction caused by wing flap extension could result in a loss of elevator effectiveness.
(9) Open left window and, if practical, scrape ice from a portion of the windshield for visibility in the landing approach.
(10) Perform a landing approach using a forward slip, if necessary, for improved visibility.
(11) Approach at 75 to 85 MPH, depending upon the amount of ice accumulation.
(12) Perform a landing in level attitude.

ROUGH ENGINE OPERATION OR LOSS OF POWER.

CARBURETOR ICING.

A gradual loss of RPM and eventual engine roughness may result from the formation of carburetor ice. To clear the ice, apply full throttle and pull the carburetor heat knob full out until the engine runs smoothly; then remove carburetor heat and readjust the throttle. If conditions require the continued use of carburetor heat in cruise flight, use the minimum amount of heat necessary to prevent ice from forming and lean the mixture slightly for smoothest engine operation.

SPARK PLUG FOULING.

A slight engine roughness in flight may be caused by one or more spark plugs becoming fouled by carbon or lead deposits. This may be verified by turning the ignition switch momentarily from BOTH to either L or R position. An obvious power loss in single ignition operation is evidence of spark plug or magneto trouble. Assuming that spark plugs are the more likely cause, lean the mixture to the normal lean setting for cruising flight. If the problem does not clear up in several minutes, determine if a richer mixture setting will produce smoother operation. If not, proceed to the nearest airport for repairs using the BOTH position of the ignition switch unless extreme roughness dictates the use of a single ignition position.

MAGNETO MALFUNCTION.

A sudden engine roughness or misfiring is usually evidence of magneto problems. Switching from BOTH to either L or R ignition switch position will identify which magneto is malfunctioning. Select different power settings and enrichen the mixture to determine if continued operation on BOTH magnetos is practicable. If not, switch to the good magneto and proceed to the nearest airport for repairs.

LOW OIL PRESSURE.

If low oil pressure is accompanied by normal oil temperature, there is a possibility the oil pressure gage or relief valve is malfunctioning. A leak in the line to the gage is not necessarily cause for an immediate precautionary landing because an orifice in this line will prevent a sudden loss of oil from the engine sump. However, a landing at the nearest airport would be advisable to inspect the source of trouble.

If a total loss of oil pressure is accompanied by a rise in oil temperature, there is good reason to suspect an engine failure is imminent. Reduce engine power immediately and select a suitable forced landing field. Leave the engine running at low power during the approach, using only the minimum power required to reach the desired touchdown spot.

ELECTRICAL POWER SUPPLY SYSTEM MALFUNCTIONS.

Malfunctions in the electrical power supply system can be detected by periodic monitoring of the ammeter and over-voltage warning light; however, the cause of these malfunctions is usually difficult to determine. A broken alternator drive belt or wiring is most likely the cause of alternator failures, although other factors could cause the problem. A damaged or improperly adjusted voltage regulator can also cause malfunctions. Problems of this nature constitute an electrical emergency and should be dealt with immediately. Electrical power malfunctions usually fall into two categories: excessive rate of charge and insufficient rate of charge.

The paragraphs below describe the recommended remedy for each situation.

EXCESSIVE RATE OF CHARGE.

After engine starting and heavy electrical usage at low engine speeds (such as extended taxiing) the battery condition will be low enough to accept above normal charging during the initial part of a flight. However, after thirty minutes of cruising flight, the ammeter should be indicating less than two needle widths of charging current. If the charging rate were to remain above this value on a long flight, the battery would overheat and evaporate the electrolyte at an excessive rate. Electronic components in the electrical system could be adversely affected by higher than normal voltage if a faulty voltage regulator setting is causing the overcharging. To preclude these possibilities, an over-voltage sensor will automatically shut down the alternator and the over-voltage warning light will illuminate if the charge voltage reaches approximately 16 volts. Assuming that the malfunction was only momentary, an attempt should be made to reactivate the alternator system. To do this, turn both sides of the master switch off and then on again. If the problem no longer exists, normal alternator charging will resume and the warning light will go off. If the light comes on again, a malfunction is confirmed. In this event, the flight should be terminated and/or the current drain on the battery minimized because the battery can supply the electrical system for only a limited period of time. If the emergency occurs at night, power must be conserved for later use of the landing light and flaps during landing.

INSUFFICIENT RATE OF CHARGE.

If the ammeter indicates a continuous discharge rate in flight, the alternator is not supplying power to the system and should be shut down since the alternator field circuit may be placing an unnecessary load on the system. All non-essential equipment should be turned off and the flight terminated as soon as practical.

EMERGENCY LOCATOR TRANSMITTER (ELT).

The ELT consists of a self-contained dual-frequency radio transmitter and battery power supply, and is activated by an impact of 5g or more as may be experienced in a crash landing. The ELT emits an omni-directional signal on the international distress frequencies of 121.5 and 243.0 MHz. General aviation and commercial aircraft, the FAA, and CAP

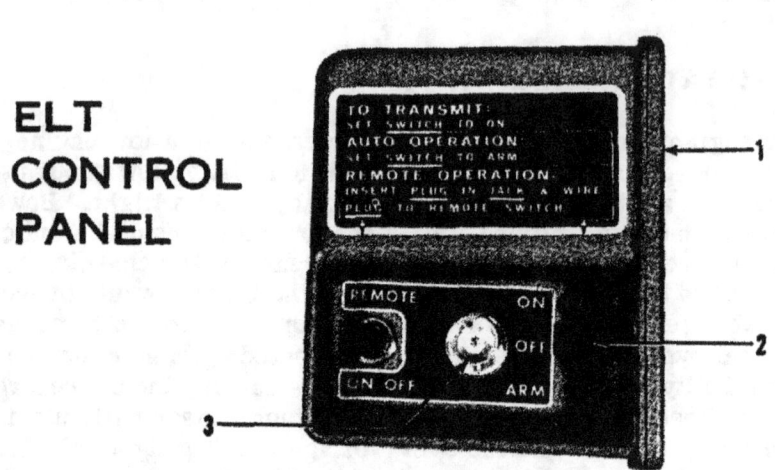

1. COVER - Removable for access to battery.

2. FUNCTION SELECTOR SWITCH (3-position toggle switch):

   ON - Activates transmitter instantly. Used for test purposes and if "g" switch is inoperative.

   OFF - Deactivates transmitter. Used during shipping, storage and following rescue.

   ARM - Activates transmitter only when "g" switch receives 5g or more impact.

3. ANTENNA RECEPTACLE - Connection to antenna mounted on top of the tailcone.

Figure 3-1.

monitor 121.5 MHz, and 243.0 MHz is monitored by the military. Following a crash landing, the ELT will provide line-of-sight transmission up to 100 miles at 10,000 feet. The duration of ELT transmissions is affected by ambient temperature. At temperatures of +70° to +130°F, continuous transmission for 115 hours can be expected; a temperature of -40°F will shorten the duration to 70 hours.

The ELT is readily identified as a bright orange unit mounted behind a cover in the aft baggage compartment on the right side of the fuselage.

To gain access to the unit, pull out on the black fasteners on the bottom of the cover and remove the cover. The ELT is operated by a control panel at the forward facing end of the unit. (see figure 3-1).

ELT OPERATION.

(1) NORMAL OPERATION: As long as the function selector switch remains in the ARM position, the ELT automatically activates following an impact of 5 g or more over a short period of time.

(2) ELT FAILURE: If "g" switch actuation is questioned following a minor crash landing, gain access to the ELT and place the function selector switch in the ON position.

(3) PRIOR TO SIGHTING RESCUE AIRCRAFT: Conserve aircraft battery. Do not activate radio transceiver.

(4) AFTER SIGHTING RESCUE AIRCRAFT: Place ELT function selector switch in the OFF position, preventing radio interference. Attempt contact with rescue aircraft with the radio transceiver set to a frequency of 121.5 MHz. If no contact is established, return the function selector switch to ON immediately.

(5) FOLLOWING RESCUE: Place ELT function selector switch in the OFF position, terminating emergency transmissions.

(6) INADVERTENT ACTIVATION: Following a lightning strike or an exceptionally hard landing, the ELT may activate although no emergency exists. Select 121.5 MHz on your radio transceiver. If the ELT can be heard transmitting, place the function selector switch in the OFF position; then immediately return the switch to ARM.

Section IV

OPERATING LIMITATIONS

OPERATIONS AUTHORIZED.

Your Cessna exceeds the requirements of airworthiness as set forth by the United States Government, and is certificated under FAA Type Certificate No. 3A12 as Cessna Model No. 172M.

The aircraft may be equipped for day, night, VFR, or IFR operation. Your Cessna Dealer will be happy to assist you in selecting equipment best suited to your needs.

Your aircraft must be operated in accordance with all FAA-approved markings and placards in the aircraft. If there is any information in this section which contradicts the FAA-approved markings and placards, it is to be disregarded.

MANEUVERS - NORMAL CATEGORY.

This aircraft is certificated in both the normal and utility category. The normal category is applicable to aircraft intended for non-aerobatic operations. These include any maneuvers incidental to normal flying, stalls (except whip stalls) and turns in which the angle of bank is not more than 60°. In connection with the foregoing, the following gross weight and flight load factors apply:

Gross Weight . . . . 2300 lbs
Flight Load Factor
   *Flaps Up . . . . +3.8   -1.52
   *Flaps Down . . . . +3.0

    *The design load factors are 150% of the above, and in all cases, the structure meets or exceeds design loads.

MANEUVERS - UTILITY CATEGORY.

This aircraft is not designed for purely aerobatic flight. However, in the acquisition of various certificates such as commercial pilot, instrument pilot and flight instructor, certain maneuvers are required by the FAA. All of these maneuvers are permitted in this aircraft when operated in the utility category. In connection with the utility category, the following gross weight and flight load factors apply, with maximum entry speeds for maneuvers as shown:

```
Gross Weight  . . . . . . . . . . . . . . . . 2000 lbs
Flight Load Factor
    Flaps Up   . . . . . . . . . . . . . . . . +4.4        -1.76
    Flaps Down . . . . . . . . . . . . . . . . +3.0
```

In the utility category, the baggage compartment and rear seat must not be occupied. No aerobatic maneuvers are approved except those listed below:

MANEUVER	RECOMMENDED ENTRY SPEED*
Chandelles	120 mph (104 knots)
Lazy Eights	120 mph (104 knots)
Steep Turns	112 mph (97 knots)
Spins	Slow Deceleration
Stalls (Except Whip Stalls)	Slow Deceleration

*Abrupt use of the controls is prohibited above 112 MPH.

Aerobatics that may impose high loads should not be attempted. The important thing to bear in mind in flight maneuvers is that the aircraft is clean in aerodynamic design and will build up speed quickly with the nose down. Proper speed control is an essential requirement for execution of any maneuver, and care should always be exercised to avoid excessive speed which in turn can impose excessive loads. In the execution of all maneuvers, avoid abrupt use of controls. Intentional spins with flaps extended are prohibited.

AIRSPEED LIMITATIONS (CAS).

The following is a list of the certificated calibrated airspeed (CAS) limitations for the aircraft.

Never Exceed Speed (glide or dive, smooth air)	182 MPH
Maximum Structural Cruising Speed	145 MPH
Maximum Speed, Flaps Extended	100 MPH
*Maneuvering Speed	112 MPH

*The maximum speed at which you may use abrupt control travel.

AIRSPEED INDICATOR MARKINGS.

The following is a list of the certificated calibrated airspeed markings (CAS) for the aircraft.

Never Exceed (glide or dive, smooth air)	182 MPH (red line)
Caution Range	145-182 MPH (yellow arc)
Normal Operating Range	61-145 MPH (green arc)
Flap Operating Range	54-100 MPH (white arc)

ENGINE OPERATION LIMITATIONS.

Power and Speed . . . . 150 BHP at 2700 RPM

ENGINE INSTRUMENT MARKINGS.

OIL TEMPERATURE GAGE.
Normal Operating Range	Green Arc
Maximum Allowable	245°F (red line)

OIL PRESSURE GAGE.
Minimum Idling	25 psi (red line)
Normal Operating Range	60-90 psi (green arc)
Maximum	100 psi (red line)

FUEL QUANTITY INDICATORS.
    Empty (2.0 gallons unusable each tank) . . . . E (red line)

TACHOMETER.
    Normal Operating Range:
        At sea level . . . . 2200-2500 RPM (inner green arc)
        At 5000 feet . . . . 2200-2600 RPM (middle green arc)
        At 10,000 feet . . . . 2200-2700 RPM (outer green arc)
    Maximum Allowable . . . . 2700 RPM (red line)

CARBURETOR AIR TEMPERATURE GAGE (OPT).
    Icing Range . . . . -15° to 5°C (yellow arc)

WEIGHT AND BALANCE.

The following information will enable you to operate your Cessna within the prescribed weight and center of gravity limitations. To figure weight and balance, use the Sample Loading Problem, Loading Graph, and Center of Gravity Moment Envelope as follows:

Take the licensed empty weight and moment from appropriate weight and balance records carried in your aircraft, and write them down in the column titled YOUR AIRPLANE on the Sample Loading Problem.

NOTE

The licensed empty weight and moment are recorded on the Weight and Balance and Installed Equipment Data sheet, or on revised weight and balance records, and are included in the aircraft file. In addition to the licensed empty weight and moment noted on these records, the c.g. arm (fuselage station) is also shown, but need not be used on the Sample Loading Problem. The moment which is shown must be divided by 1000 and this value used as the moment/1000 on the loading problem.

Use the Loading Graph to determine the moment/1000 for each additional item to be carried, then list these on the loading problem.

NOTE

Loading Graph information for the pilot, passengers and baggage is based on seats positioned for average occupants and baggage loaded in the center of the baggage area as shown on the Loading Arrangements diagram. For loadings which may differ from these, the Sample Loading Problem lists fuselage stations for these items to indicate their forward and aft c.g. range limitation (seat travel or baggage area limitation). Additional moment calculations, based on the actual weight and c.g. arm (fuselage station) of the item being loaded, must be made if the position of the load is different from that shown on the Loading Graph.

Total the weights and moments/1000 and plot these values on the Center of Gravity Moment Envelope to determine whether the point falls within the envelope, and if the loading is acceptable.

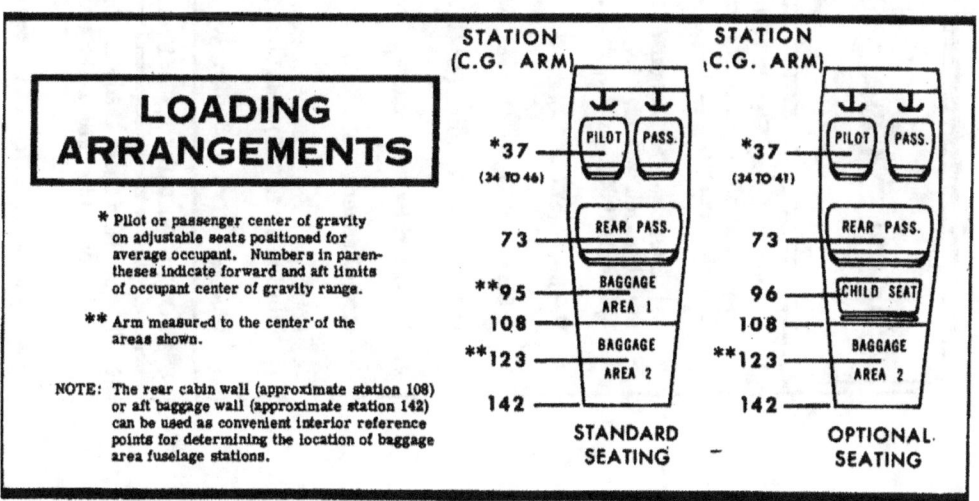

4-5

	SAMPLE AIRPLANE		YOUR AIRPLANE	
SAMPLE LOADING PROBLEM	Weight (lbs.)	Moment (lb.-ins. /1000)	Weight (lbs.)	Moment (lb.-ins. /1000)
1. Licensed Empty Weight (Use the data pertaining to your airplane as it is presently equipped. Includes unusable fuel.)	1366	53.8		
2. Oil (8 Qts. - The weight of full oil may be used for all calculations. 8 Qts. = 15 Lbs. at -0.2 Moment/1000)	15	-0.2	15	-0.2
3. Usable Fuel (At 6 Lbs./Gal.)				
Standard Tanks (38 Gal. Maximum)	228	10.9		
Long Range Tanks (48 Gal. Maximum)				
4. Pilot and Front Passenger (Station 34 to 46) . . .	340	12.6		
5. Rear Passengers	340	24.8		
6.*Baggage Area 1 or Passenger on Child's Seat (Station 82 to 108) 120 Lbs. Max.	11	1.0		
7.*Baggage Area 2 (Station 108 to 142) 50 Lbs. Max. .				
8. TOTAL WEIGHT AND MOMENT	2300	102.9		
9. Locate this point (2300 at 102.9) on the Center of Gravity Moment Envelope, and since this point falls within the envelope, the loading is acceptable.				

NOTE

*The maximum allowable combined weight capacity for baggage areas 1 and 2 is 120 lbs.

4-6

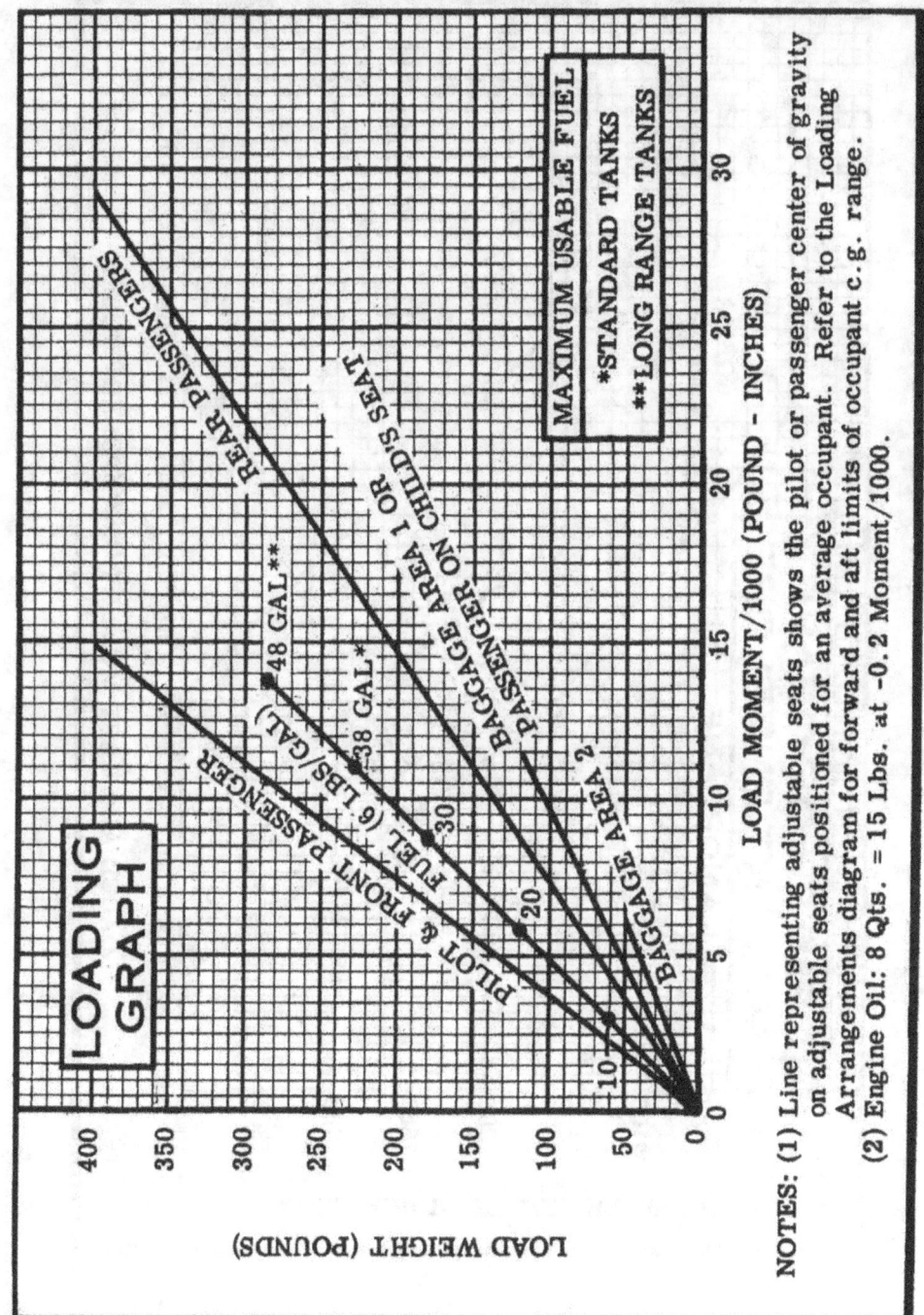

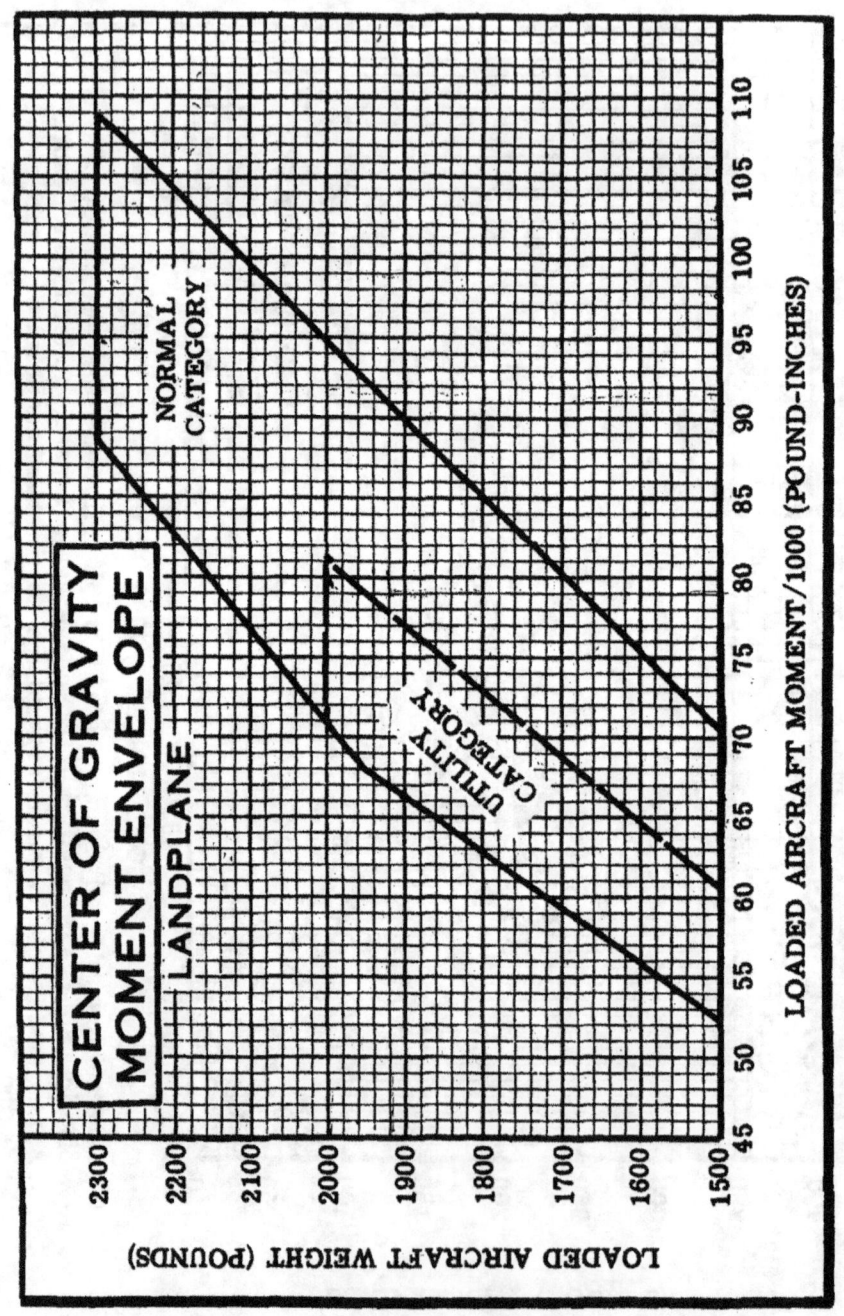

Section V

CARE OF THE AIRPLANE

If your airplane is to retain that new plane performance and dependability, certain inspection and maintenance requirements must be followed. It is wise to follow a planned schedule of lubrication and preventive maintenance based on climatic and flying conditions encountered in your locality.

Keep in touch with your Cessna Dealer and take advantage of his knowledge and experience. He knows your airplane and how to maintain it. He will remind you when lubrications and oil changes are necessary, and about other seasonal and periodic services.

GROUND HANDLING.

The airplane is most easily and safely maneuvered by hand with the tow-bar attached to the nose wheel. When towing with a vehicle, do not exceed the nose gear turning angle of 30° either side of center, or damage to the gear will result. If the airplane is towed or pushed over a rough surface during hangaring, watch that the normal cushioning action of the nose strut does not cause excessive vertical movement of the tail and the resulting contact with low hangar doors or structure. A flat nose wheel tire or deflated strut will also increase tail height.

MOORING YOUR AIRPLANE.

Proper tie-down procedure is your best precaution against damage to your parked airplane by gusty or strong winds. To tie down your airplane securely, proceed as follows:

(1) Set the parking brake and install the control wheel lock.
(2) Tie sufficiently strong ropes or chains (700 pounds tensile strength) to wing, tail and nose tie-down rings and secure each rope to a ramp tie-down.

(3) Install a surface control lock over the fin and rudder.
(4) Install a pitot tube cover.

WINDSHIELD - WINDOWS.

The plastic windshield and windows should be cleaned with an aircraft windshield cleaner. Apply the cleaner sparingly with soft cloths, and rub with moderate pressure until all dirt, oil scum and bug stains are removed. Allow the cleaner to dry, then wipe it off with soft flannel cloths.

If a windshield cleaner is not available, the plastic can be cleaned with soft cloths moistened with Stoddard solvent to remove oil and grease.

NOTE

Never use gasoline, benzine, alcohol, acetone, carbon tetrachloride, fire extinguisher or anti-ice fluid, lacquer thinner or glass cleaner to clean the plastic. These materials will attack the plastic and may cause it to craze.

Follow by carefully washing with a mild detergent and plenty of water. Rinse thoroughly, then dry with a clean moist chamois. Do not rub the plastic with a dry cloth since this builds up an electrostatic charge which attracts dust. Waxing with a good commercial wax will finish the cleaning job. A thin, even coat of wax, polished out by hand with clean soft flannel cloths, will fill in minor scratches and help prevent further scratching.

Do not use a canvas cover on the windshield unless freezing rain or sleet is anticipated since the cover may scratch the plastic surface.

PAINTED SURFACES.

The painted exterior surfaces of your new Cessna have a durable, long lasting finish and, under normal conditions, require no polishing or buffing. Approximately 15 days are required for the paint to cure completely; in most cases, the curing period will have been completed prior to delivery of the airplane. In the event that polishing or buffing is required within the curing period, it is recommended that the work be done by someone experienced in handling uncured paint. Any Cessna Dealer can accomplish this work.

Generally, the painted surfaces can be kept bright by washing with water and mild soap, followed by a rinse with water and drying with cloths or a chamois. Harsh or abrasive soaps or detergents which cause corrosion or scratches should never be used. Remove stubborn oil and grease with a cloth moistened with Stoddard solvent.

Waxing is unnecessary to keep the painted surfaces bright. However, if desired, the airplane may be waxed with a good automotive wax. A heavier coating of wax on the leading edges of the wings and tail and on the engine nose cap and propeller spinner will help reduce the abrasion encountered in these areas.

When the airplane is parked outside in cold climates and it is necessary to remove ice before flight, care should be taken to protect the painted surfaces during ice removal with chemical liquids. A 50-50 solution of isopropyl alcohol and water will satisfactorily remove ice accumulations without damaging the paint. A solution with more than 50% alcohol is harmful and should be avoided. While applying the de-icing solution, keep it away from the windshield and cabin windows since the alcohol will attack the plastic and may cause it to craze.

ALUMINUM SURFACES.

The clad aluminum surfaces of your Cessna may be washed with clear water to remove dirt; oil and grease may be removed with gasoline, naphtha, carbon tetrachloride or other non-alkaline solvents. Dulled aluminum surfaces may be cleaned effectively with an aircraft aluminum polish.

After cleaning, and periodically thereafter, waxing with a good automotive wax will preserve the bright appearance and retard corrosion. Regular waxing is especially recommended for airplanes operated in salt water areas as a protection against corrosion.

PROPELLER CARE.

Preflight inspection of propeller blades for nicks, and wiping them occasionally with an oily cloth to clean off grass and bug stains will assure long, trouble-free service. Small nicks on the propeller, particularly near the tips and on the leading edges, should be dressed out as soon as possible since these nicks produce stress concentrations, and if ignored, may result in cracks. Never use an alkaline cleaner on the blades; remove grease and dirt with carbon tetrachloride or Stoddard solvent.

INTERIOR CARE.

To remove dust and loose dirt from the upholstery and carpet, clean the interior regularly with a vacuum cleaner.

Blot up any spilled liquid promptly, with cleansing tissue or rags. Don't pat the spot; press the blotting material firmly and hold it for several seconds. Continue blotting until no more liquid is taken up. Scrape off sticky materials with a dull knife, then spot-clean the area.

Oily spots may be cleaned with household spot removers, used sparingly. Before using any solvent, read the instructions on the container and test it on an obscure place on the fabric to be cleaned. Never saturate the fabric with a volatile solvent; it may damage the padding and backing materials.

Soiled upholstery and carpet may be cleaned with foam-type detergent, used according to the manufacturer's instructions. To minimize wetting the fabric, keep the foam as dry as possible and remove it with a vacuum cleaner.

If your airplane is equipped with leather seating, cleaning of the seats is accomplished using a soft cloth or sponge dipped in mild soap suds. The soap suds, used sparingly, will remove traces of dirt and grease. The soap should be removed with a clean damp cloth.

The plastic trim, headliner, instrument panel and control knobs need only be wiped off with a damp cloth. Oil and grease on the control wheel and control knobs can be removed with a cloth moistened with Stoddard solvent. Volatile solvents, such as mentioned in paragraphs on care of the windshield, must never be used since they soften and craze the plastic

MAA PLATE/FINISH AND TRIM PLATE.

Information concerning the Type Certificate Number (TC), Production Certificate Number (PC), Model Number and Serial Number of your particular aircraft can be found on the MAA (Manufacturers Aircraft Association) plate located on the lower part of the left forward door post.

A Finish and Trim plate contains a code describing the interior color scheme and exterior paint combination of the aircraft. The code may be used in conjunction with an applicable Parts Catalog if finish and trim information is needed. This plate is located adjacent to the MAA plate on the left forward door post.

AIRCRAFT FILE.

There are miscellaneous data, information and licenses that are a part of the aircraft file. The following is a checklist for that file. In addition, a periodic check should be made of the latest Federal Aviation Regulations to ensure that all data requirements are met.

A. To be displayed in the aircraft at all times:

(1) Aircraft Airworthiness Certificate (FAA Form 8100-2).
(2) Aircraft Registration Certificate (FAA Form 8050-3).
(3) Aircraft Radio Station License, if transmitter installed (FCC Form 556).

B. To be carried in the aircraft at all times:

(1) Weight and Balance, and associated papers (latest copy of the Repair and Alteration Form, FAA Form 337, if applicable).
(2) Aircraft Equipment List.

C. To be made available upon request:

(1) Aircraft Log Book.
(2) Engine Log Book.

Most of the items listed are required by the United States Federal Aviation Regulations. Since the regulations of other nations may require other documents and data, owners of exported aircraft should check with their own aviation officials to determine their individual requirements.

Cessna recommends that these items, plus the Owner's Manual, Power Computer, Pilot's Checklist, Customer Care Program book and Customer Care Card, be carried in the aircraft at all times.

FLYABLE STORAGE.

Aircraft placed in non-operational storage for a maximum of 30 days or those which receive only intermittent operational use for the first 25 hours are considered in flyable storage status. Every seventh day during these periods, the propeller should be rotated by hand through five revolutions. This action "limbers" the oil and prevents any accumulation of corrosion on engine cylinder walls.

IMPORTANT

For maximum safety, check that the ignition switch is OFF, the throttle is closed, the mixture control is in the idle cut-off position, and the airplane is secured before rotating the propeller by hand. Do not stand within the arc of the propeller blades while turning the propeller.

After 30 days, the aircraft should be flown for 30 minutes or a ground runup should be made just long enough to produce an oil temperature within the lower green arc range. Excessive ground runup should be avoided.

Engine runup also helps to eliminate excessive accumulations of water in the fuel system and other air spaces in the engine. Keep fuel tanks full to minimize condensation in the tanks. Keep the battery fully charged to prevent the electrolyte from freezing in cold weather. If the aircraft is to be stored temporarily, or indefinitely, refer to the Service Manual for proper storage procedures.

INSPECTION REQUIREMENTS.

As required by Federal Aviation Regulations, all civil aircraft of U.S. registry must undergo a complete inspection (annual) each twelve calendar months. In addition to the required ANNUAL inspection, aircraft operated commercially (for hire) must have a complete inspection every 100 hours of operation.

In lieu of the above requirements, an aircraft may be inspected in accordance with a progressive inspection schedule, which allows the work load to be divided into smaller operations that can be accomplished in shorter time periods.

The CESSNA PROGRESSIVE CARE PROGRAM has been developed to provide a modern progressive inspection schedule that satisfies the complete aircraft inspection requirements of both the 100 HOUR and ANNUAL inspections as applicable to Cessna aircraft.

CESSNA PROGRESSIVE CARE.

The Cessna Progressive Care Program has been designed to help you realize maximum utilization of your aircraft at a minimum cost and downtime. Under this program, your aircraft is inspected and maintained in four operations at 50-hour intervals during a 200-hour period. The operations are recycled each 200 hours and are recorded in a specially provided Aircraft Inspection Log as each operation is conducted.

The Cessna Aircraft Company recommends Progressive Care for aircraft that are being flown 200 hours or more per year, and the 100-hour inspection for all other aircraft. The procedures for the Progressive Care Program and the 100-hour inspection have been carefully worked out by the factory and are followed by the Cessna Dealer Organization. The complete familiarity of Cessna Dealers with Cessna equipment and factory-approved procedures provides the highest level of service possible at lower cost to Cessna owners.

CESSNA CUSTOMER CARE PROGRAM.

Specific benefits and provisions of the CESSNA WARRANTY plus other important benefits for you are contained in your CUSTOMER CARE PROGRAM book supplied with your aircraft. You will want to thoroughly review your Customer Care Program book and keep it in your aircraft at all times.

Coupons attached to the Program book entitle you to an initial inspection and either a Progressive Care Operation No. 1 or the first 100-hour inspection within the first 6 months of ownership at no charge to you. If you take delivery from your Dealer, the initial inspection will have been performed before delivery of the aircraft to you. If you pick up your aircraft at the factory, plan to take it to your Dealer reasonably soon after you take delivery, so the initial inspection may be performed allowing the Dealer to make any minor adjustments which may be necessary.

You will also want to return to your Dealer either at 50 hours for your first Progressive Care Operation, or at 100 hours for your first 100-hour inspection depending on which program you choose to establish for your aircraft. While these important inspections will be performed for you by any Cessna Dealer, in most cases you will prefer to have the Dealer from whom you purchased the aircraft accomplish this work.

SERVICING REQUIREMENTS.

For quick and ready reference, quantities, materials, and specifications for frequently used service items (such as fuel, oil, etc.) are shown on the inside back cover of this manual.

In addition to the EXTERIOR INSPECTION covered in Section I, COMPLETE servicing, inspection, and test requirements for your aircraft are detailed in the aircraft Service Manual. The Service Manual outlines all items which require attention at 50, 100, and 200 hour intervals plus those items which require servicing, inspection, and/or testing at special intervals.

Since Cessna Dealers conduct all service, inspection, and test procedures in accordance with applicable Service Manual, it is recommended that you contact your Dealer concerning these requirements and begin scheduling your aircraft for service at the recommended intervals.

Cessna Progressive Care ensures that these requirements are accomplished at the required intervals to comply with the 100-hour or ANNUAL inspection as previously covered.

Depending on various flight operations, your local Government Aviation Agency may require additional service, inspections, or tests. For these regulatory requirements, owners should check with local aviation officials where the aircraft is being operated.

OWNER FOLLOW-UP SYSTEM.

Your Cessna Dealer has an Owner Follow-Up System to notify you when he receives information that applies to your Cessna. In addition, if you wish, you may choose to receive similar notification, in the form of Service Letters, directly from the Cessna Customer Services Department.

A subscription form is supplied in your Customer Care Program book for your use, should you choose to request this service. Your Cessna Dealer will be glad to supply you with details concerning these follow-up programs, and stands ready, through his Service Department, to supply you with fast, efficient, low-cost service.

PUBLICATIONS.

Various publications and flight operation aids are furnished in the aircraft when delivered from the factory. These items are listed below.

- CUSTOMER CARE PROGRAM BOOK

- OWNER'S MANUALS FOR YOUR
    AIRCRAFT
    AVIONICS AND AUTOPILOT

- POWER COMPUTER

- SALES AND SERVICE DEALER DIRECTORY

The following additional publications, plus many other supplies that are applicable to your aircraft, are available from your Cessna Dealer.

- SERVICE MANUALS AND PARTS CATALOGS FOR YOUR
    AIRCRAFT
    ENGINE AND ACCESSORIES
    AVIONICS AND AUTOPILOT

Your Cessna Dealer has a current catalog of all Customer Services Supplies that are available, many of which he keeps on hand. Supplies which are not in stock, he will be happy to order for you.

Section VI

OPERATIONAL DATA

The operational data shown on the following pages are compiled from actual tests with the aircraft and engine in good condition and using average piloting technique. You will find this data a valuable aid when planning your flights.

A power setting selected from the range chart usually will be more efficient than a random setting, since it will permit you to estimate your fuel consumption more accurately. You will find that using the charts and your Power Computer will pay dividends in overall efficiency.

Cruise and range performance shown in this section is based on the use of a McCauley 1C160/DTM7553 propeller and a standard equipped Skyhawk. Other conditions for the performance data are shown in the chart headings. Allowances for fuel reserve, headwinds, take-off and climb, and variations in mixture leaning technique should be made and are in addition to those shown on the chart. Other indeterminate variables such as carburetor metering characteristics, engine and propeller conditions, externally-mounted optional equipment and turbulence of the atmosphere may account for variations of 10% or more in maximum range.

Remember that the charts contained herein are based on standard day conditions. For more precise power, fuel consumption, and endurance information, consult the Cessna Power Computer supplied with your aircraft. With the Power Computer, you can easily take into account temperature variations from standard at any flight altitude.

AIRSPEED CORRECTION TABLE

	IAS	40	50	60	70	80	90	100	110	120	130	140
FLAPS UP	CAS	53	58	64	72	79	88	97	107	117	127	137
FLAPS DOWN	CAS	49	55	63	72	81	90	100	•	•	•	•

Figure 6-1.

STALL SPEEDS – MPH CAS

	CONDITION	ANGLE OF BANK			
		0°	20°	40°	60°
2300 LBS. GROSS WEIGHT	FLAPS UP	57	59	65	81
	FLAPS 10° 20° *(handwritten)*	52 50 *(handwritten)*	54 52 *(handwritten)*	59	74
	FLAPS 40°	49	51	56	69

POWER OFF — AFT CG

Figure 6-2.

TAKE-OFF DATA

TAKE-OFF DISTANCE FROM HARD SURFACE RUNWAY WITH FLAPS UP

GROSS WEIGHT POUNDS	IAS AT 50' MPH	HEAD WIND KNOTS	AT SEA LEVEL & 59°F		AT 2500 FT. & 50°F		AT 5000 FT. & 41°F		AT 7500 FT. & 32°F	
			GROUND RUN	TOTAL TO CLEAR 50 FT OBS	GROUND RUN	TOTAL TO CLEAR 50 FT OBS	GROUND RUN	TOTAL TO CLEAR 50 FT OBS	GROUND RUN	TOTAL TO CLEAR 50 FT OBS
2300	68	0	865	1525	1040	1910	1255	2480	1565	3855
		10	615	1170	750	1485	920	1955	1160	3110
		20	405	850	505	1100	630	1480	810	2425
2000	63	0	630	1095	755	1325	905	1625	1120	2155
		10	435	820	530	1005	645	1250	810	1685
		20	275	580	340	720	425	910	595	1255
1700	58	0	435	780	520	920	625	1095	765	1370
		10	290	570	355	680	430	820	535	1040
		20	175	385	215	470	270	575	345	745

NOTES:
1. Increase distance 10% for each 25°F. above standard temperature for particular altitude.
2. For operation on a dry, grass runway, increase distances (both "ground run" and "total to clear 50 ft. obstacle") by 7% of the "total to clear 50 ft. obstacle" figure.

MAXIMUM RATE-OF-CLIMB DATA

GROSS WEIGHT POUNDS	AT SEA LEVEL & 59°F			AT 5000 FT. & 41°F			AT 10,000 FT. & 23°F			AT 15,000 FT. & 5°F		
	IAS MPH	RATE OF CLIMB FT/MIN	GAL. OF FUEL USED	IAS MPH	RATE OF CLIMB FT/MIN	FROM S.L. FUEL USED	IAS MPH	RATE OF CLIMB FT/MIN	FROM S.L. FUEL USED	IAS MPH	RATE OF CLIMB FT/MIN	FROM S.L. FUEL USED
2300	91	645	1.0	85	435	2.6	80	230	4.8	73	20	11.5
2000	88	840	1.0	81	610	2.2	75	380	3.6	68	155	6.3
1700	83	1085	1.0	77	825	1.9	70	570	2.9	64	315	4.4

NOTES:
1. Flaps up, full throttle, mixture leaned for smooth operation above 3000 ft.
2. Fuel used includes warm up and take-off allowance.
3. For hot weather, decrease rate of climb 20 ft./min. for each 10°F above standard day temperature for particular altitude.

Figure 6-3.

CRUISE PERFORMANCE
SKYHAWK

Gross Weight - 2300 Lbs.
Standard Conditions
Zero Wind   Lean Mixture

NOTE: Maximum cruise is normally limited to 75% power. Cruise speeds for the standard Model 172 are 1 to 3 MPH lower than shown with the maximum difference occurring at higher powers.

ALTITUDE	RPM	% BHP	TAS MPH	GAL/ HOUR	38 GAL (NO RESERVE)		48 GAL (NO RESERVE)	
					ENDR. HOURS	RANGE MILES	ENDR. HOURS	RANGE MILES
2500	2700	87	139	9.6	3.9	545	5.0	690
	2600	78	133	8.6	4.4	590	5.6	745
	2500	70	128	7.7	4.9	630	6.2	795
	2400	63	122	7.1	5.3	655	6.7	825
	2300	57	116	6.6	5.7	665	7.2	840
	2200	51	109	6.2	6.1	665	7.7	840
5000	2700	81	138	8.9	4.3	585	5.4	740
	2600	73	133	8.1	4.7	630	6.0	795
	2500	66	128	7.4	5.1	655	6.5	830
	2400	60	121	6.8	5.6	675	7.0	850
	2300	54	114	6.4	5.9	675	7.5	855
	2200	48	107	6.0	6.3	675	8.0	850
7500	2700	76	138	8.4	4.5	630	5.7	795
	2600	69	133	7.6	5.0	660	6.3	835
	2500	63	126	7.1	5.4	675	6.8	855
	2400	57	119	6.6	5.8	685	7.3	865
	2300	51	112	6.2	6.1	685	7.8	865
10,000	2700	72	138	7.9	4.8	665	6.1	840
	2600	66	131	7.3	5.2	685	6.6	860
	2500	59	124	6.8	5.6	695	7.1	875
	2400	54	117	6.4	6.0	700	7.5	880
	2300	48	110	6.0	6.3	700	8.0	880
12,500	2650	65	132	7.2	5.3	695	6.6	880
	2500	56	122	6.5	5.8	710	7.3	895
	2400	51	115	6.2	6.2	710	7.8	895

Figure 6-4.

LANDING DATA

LANDING DISTANCE ON HARD SURFACE RUNWAY
NO WIND – 40° FLAPS – POWER OFF

GROSS WEIGHT LBS.	APPROACH IAS MPH	AT SEA LEVEL & 59°F		AT 2500 FT. & 50°F		AT 5000 FT. & 41°F		AT 7500 FT. & 32°F	
		GROUND ROLL	TOTAL TO CLEAR 50' OBS.	GROUND ROLL	TOTAL TO CLEAR 50' OBS.	GROUND ROLL	TOTAL TO CLEAR 50' OBS.	GROUND ROLL	TOTAL TO CLEAR 50' OBS.
2300	70	520	1250	560	1310	605	1385	650	1455

NOTES: 1. Reduce landing distance 10% for each 5 knot headwind.
2. For operation on a dry, grass runway, increase distances (both "ground roll" and "total to clear 50 ft. obstacle") by 20% of the "total to clear 50 ft. obstacle" figure.

Figure 6-5.

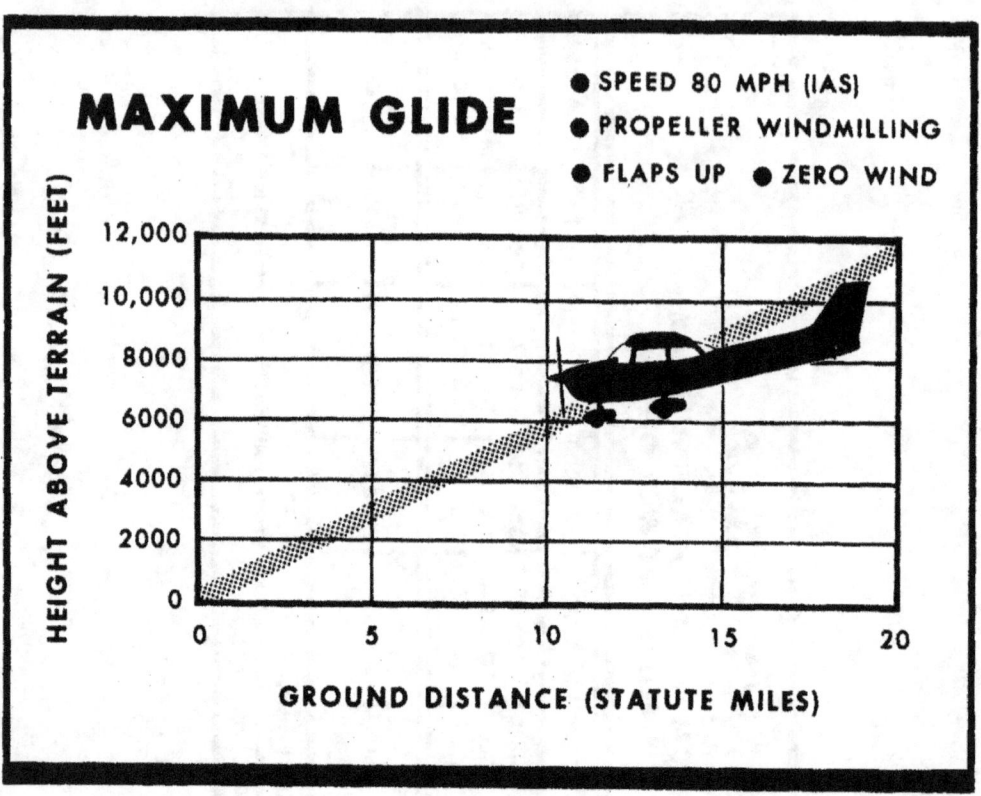

Figure 6-6.

Section VII

OPTIONAL SYSTEMS

This section contains a description, operating procedures, and performance data (when applicable) for some of the optional equipment which may be installed in your Cessna. Owner's Manual Supplements are provided to cover operation of other optional equipment systems when installed in your airplane. Contact your Cessna Dealer for a complete list of available optional equipment.

COLD WEATHER EQUIPMENT

WINTERIZATION KIT.

For continuous operation in temperatures consistently below 20°F, the Cessna winterization kit, available from your Cessna Dealer, should be installed to improve engine operation. The kit consists of two baffles which attach to the engine air intakes in the cowling, a restrictive cover plate for the oil cooler air inlet in the right rear vertical engine baffle, and insulation for the crankcase breather line. Once installed, the crankcase breather insulation is approved for permanent use in both cold and hot weather.

GROUND SERVICE PLUG RECEPTACLE.

A ground service plug receptacle may be installed to permit use of an external power source for cold weather starting and during lengthy maintenance work on the airplane electrical system (with the exception of electronic equipment).

NOTE

Electrical power for the airplane electrical circuits is provided through a split bus bar having all electronic circuits on one side of the bus and other electrical circuits on the other side of the bus. When an external power source is connected, a contactor automatically opens the circuit to the electronic portion of the split bus bar as a protection against damage to the transistors in the electronic equipment by transient voltages from the power source. Therefore, the external power source can not be used as a source of power when checking electronic components.

Just before connecting an external power source (generator type or battery cart), the master switch should be turned on.

The ground service plug receptacle circuit incorporates a polarity reversal protection. Power from the external power source will flow only if the ground service plug is correctly connected to the airplane. If the plug is accidentally connected backwards, no power will flow to the airplane's electrical system, thereby preventing any damage to electrical equipment.

The battery and external power circuits have been designed to completely eliminate the need to "jumper" across the battery contactor to close it for charging a completely "dead" battery. A special fused circuit in the external power system supplies the needed "jumper" across the contacts so that with a "dead" battery and an external power source applied, turning on the master switch will close the battery contactor.

STATIC PRESSURE ALTERNATE SOURCE VALVE.

A static pressure alternate source valve may be installed in the static system for use when the external static source is malfunctioning.

If erroneous instrument readings are suspected due to water or ice in the static pressure lines, the static pressure alternate source valve control knob located below the wing flap switch should be opened, thereby supplying static pressure from the cabin. Cabin pressures will vary, however, with open cabin ventilators or windows. The most adverse combinations will result in airspeed and altimeter variations of no more than 2 MPH and 15 feet, respectively.

RADIO SELECTOR SWITCHES

RADIO SELECTOR SWITCH OPERATION.

Operation of the radio equipment is normal as covered in the respective radio manuals. When more than one radio is installed, an audio switching system is necessary. The operation of this switching system is described below.

TRANSMITTER SELECTOR SWITCH.

The transmitter selector switch, labeled TRANS, has two positions. When two transmitters are installed, it is necessary to switch the microphone to the radio unit the pilot desires to use for transmission. This is accomplished by placing the transmitter selector switch in the position corresponding to the radio unit which is to be used. The up position selects the upper transmitter and the down position selects the lower transmitter.

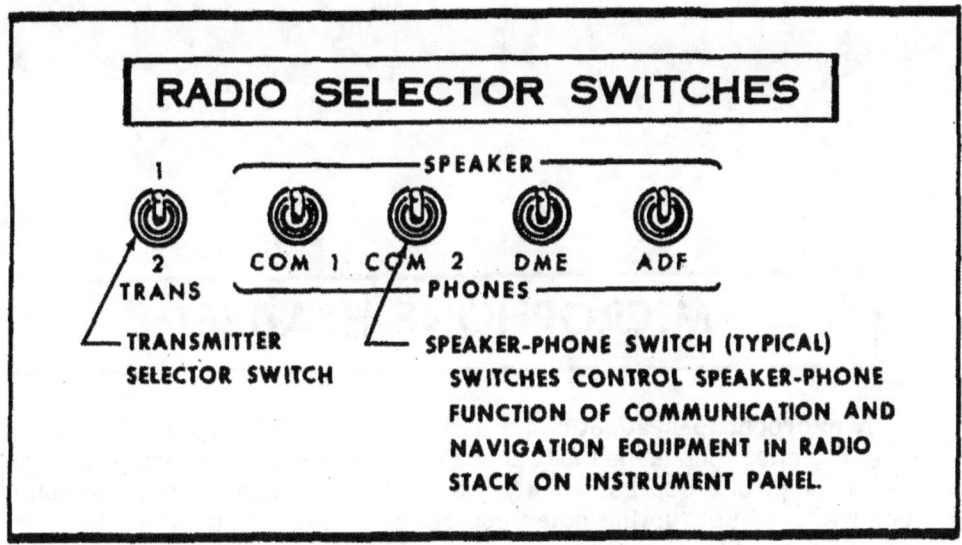

Figure 7-1.

The installation of Cessna radio equipment provides certain audio back-up capabilities and transmitter selector switch functions that the pilot should be familiar with. When the transmitter selector switch is placed in position 1 or 2, the audio amplifier of the corresponding transceiver is utilized to provide the speaker audio for all radios. If the audio amplifier in the selected transceiver fails, as evidenced by loss of speaker audio for all radios, place the transmitter selector switch in the other transceiver position. Since an audio amplifier is not utilized for headphones, a malfunctioning amplifier will not affect headphone operation.

SPEAKER PHONE SWITCHES.

The speaker-phone switches determine whether the output of the receiver in use is fed to the headphones or through the audio amplifier to the speaker. Place the switch for the desired receiving system either in the up position for speaker operation or in the down position for headphones.

MICROPHONE-HEADSET

A microphone-headset combination is offered as optional equipment. Using the microphone-headset and a microphone keying switch on the left side of the pilot's control wheel, the pilot can conduct radio communications without interrupting other control operations to handle a hand-held microphone. Also, passengers need not listen to all communications. The microphone and headset jacks are located near the lower left corner of the instrument panel.

TRUE AIRSPEED INDICATOR

A true airspeed indicator is available to replace the standard airspeed indicator in your airplane. The true airspeed indicator has a calibrated rotatable ring which works in conjunction with the airspeed indicator dial in a manner similar to the operation of a flight computer.

TO OBTAIN TRUE AIRSPEED, rotate ring until pressure altitude is aligned with outside air temperature in degrees Fahrenheit. Then read true airspeed on rotatable ring opposite airspeed needle.

NOTE

Pressure altitude should not be confused with indicated altitude. To obtain pressure altitude, set barometric scale on altimeter to "29.92" and read pressure altitude on altimeter. Be sure to return altimeter barometric scale to original barometric setting after pressure altitude has been obtained.

CARBURETOR AIR TEMPERATURE GAGE

A carburetor air temperature gage may be installed in the aircraft to help detect carburetor icing conditions. The gage is marked with a yellow arc between -15° and +5°C. The yellow arc indicates the carburetor temperature range where carburetor icing can occur; a placard on the gage reads KEEP NEEDLE OUT OF YELLOW ARC DURING POSSIBLE ICING CONDITIONS.

Visible moisture or high humidity can cause carburetor ice formation, especially in idle or low power conditions. Under cruising conditions, the formation of ice is usually slow, providing time to detect the loss of RPM caused by the ice. Carburetor icing during take-off is rare since the full-open throttle condition is less susceptible to ice obstruction.

If the carburetor air temperature gage needle moves into the yellow arc during potential carburetor icing conditions, or there is an unexplained drop in RPM, apply full carburetor heat. Upon regaining the original RPM (with heat off), determine by trial and error the minimum amount of carburetor heat required for ice-free operation.

NOTE

Carburetor heat should not be applied during take-off unless absolutely necessary to obtain smooth engine acceleration (usually in sub-zero temperatures).

OIL QUICK-DRAIN VALVE

An oil quick-drain valve is optionally offered to replace the drain plug in the oil sump drain port. The valve provides a quicker and cleaner method of draining engine oil. To drain the oil with this valve installed, slip a hose over the end of the valve, route the hose to a suitable container, then push upward on the end of the valve until it snaps into the open position. Spring clips will hold the valve open. After draining, use a screwdriver or suitable tool to snap the valve into the extended (closed) position and remove the drain hose.

ALPHABETICAL INDEX

A

After Landing, 1-6
Aircraft,
    file, 5-5
    mooring, 5-1
    securing, 1-7
Airspeed Correction Table, 6-2
Airspeed Indicator, True, 7-5
Airspeed Indicator Markings, 4-3
Airspeed Limitations, 4-3
Alternate Source Valve, Static Pressure, 7-2
Alternator Check, 2-13
Aluminum Surfaces, 5-3
Ammeter, 2-5
Authorized Operations, 4-1

B

Balked Landing, 1-6, 2-19
Before Landing, 1-6
Before Starting Engine, 1-4
Before Take-Off, 1-4, 2-12
    alternator check, 2-13
    magneto check, 2-12
    warm-up, 2-12

C

Cabin Heating, Ventilating and Defrosting System, 2-8
Capacity,
    fuel, inside back cover
    oil, inside back cover
Carburetor Air Temperature Gage, 4-4, 7-5
Carburetor Icing, 3-7

Care,
    interior, 5-4
    propeller, 5-3
Center of Gravity Moment Envelope, 4-8
Cessna Customer Care Program, 5-7
Cessna Progressive Care, 5-7
Circuit Breakers and Fuses, 2-6
Climb,
    data, 2-15
    enroute, 1-5, 2-15
    maximum rate-of-climb data chart, 6-3
    speeds, 2-15
Cold Weather Equipment, 7-1
    ground service plug receptacle, 7-1
    static pressure alternate source valve, 7-2
    winterization kit, 7-1
Cold Weather Operation, 2-19
    flight operations, 2-20
    starting, 2-18
Correction Table, Airspeed, 6-2
Crosswind Landing, 2-18
Crosswind Take-Off, 2-14
Cruise Performance Chart, 2-15, 6-4
Cruising, 1-5, 2-16

D

Diagram,
    electrical system, 2-4
    ELT control panel, 3-10
    exterior inspection, 1-2
    fuel system, 2-2

    instrument panel, 1-8
    loading arrangements, 4-5
    maximum glide, 6-6
    principal dimensions, ii
    radio selector switches, 7-3
    taxiing, 2-11
Dimensions, Principal, ii
Disorientation In Clouds, 3-5
    emergency let-downs through clouds, 3-5
    executing 180° turn in clouds, 3-5
    recovery from spiral dive, 3-6
Ditching, 3-3

E

Electrical Fire in Flight, 3-4
Electrical Power Supply System Malfunctions, 3-8
    excessive rate of charge, 3-9
    insufficient rate of charge, 3-9
Electrical System, 2-3
    ammeter, 2-5
    circuit breakers and fuses, 2-6
    ground service plug receptacle, 7-1
    master switch, 2-4, 2-5
    over-voltage sensor and warning light, 2-5
    schematic, 2-4
Emergency Landing without Engine Power, 3-2
Emergency Let-Downs Through Clouds, 3-5
Emergency Locator Transmitter (ELT), 3-9
    ELT operation, 3-11
Empty Weight, inside front cover
Engine,
    before starting, 1-4
    fire during start on ground, 3-3
    fire in flight, 3-4
    instrument markings, 4-3
    oil, inside back cover
    operation limitations, 4-3
    rough operation or loss of power, 3-7
    starting, 1-4, 2-10
Engine Failure, 3-1
    after take-off, 3-1
    during flight, 3-1
Enroute Climb, 1-5, 2-15
Equipment, Cold Weather, 7-1
Excessive Rate of Electrical Charge, 3-9
Executing 180° Turn in Clouds, 3-5
Exterior Inspection Diagram, 1-2
Exterior Lighting, 2-6

F

File, Aircraft, 5-5
Finish and Trim Plate, MAA Plate, 5-4
Fires, 3-3
    electrical fire in flight, 3-4
    engine fire during start on ground, 3-3
    engine fire in flight, 3-4
Flight in Icing Conditions, 3-6
Flyable Storage, 5-6
Forced Landings, 3-2
    ditching, 3-3
    emergency landing without engine power, 3-2
    precautionary landing with engine power, 3-2
Fuel System, 2-1
    capacity, inside back cover
    fuel grade, inside back cover
    fuel quantity indicators, 4-4
    long range fuel tanks, 2-3
    quick-drain valves, 2-3
    schematic, 2-2
Fuses and Circuit Breakers, 2-6

G

Graph, Loading, 4-7
Gross Weight, inside front cover
Ground Handling, 5-1
Ground Service Plug Receptacle, 7-1

H

Handling Airplane on Ground, 5-1
Harnesses, Shoulder, 2-9
Headset-Microphone, 7-4
Heating, Ventilating and Defrosting System, Cabin, 2-8
Hot Weather Operation, 2-21

I

Indicator, Fuel Quantity, 4-4
Indicator, True Airspeed, 7-5
Inspection Requirements, 5-6
Instrument Markings, Engine, 4-3
Instrument Panel Diagram, 1-8
Insufficient Rate of Electrical Charge, 3-9
Integrated Seat Belt/Shoulder Harnesses With Inertia Reel, 2-9
Interior Care, 5-4
Interior Lighting, 2-7
Inertia Reel, Integrated Seat Belt/Shoulder Harnesses, 2-9

L

Landings, 2-18
   after, 1-6
   balked, 1-6, 2-18
   before, 1-6
   crosswind, 2-18
   distance table, 6-5
   forced, 3-2
   normal, 1-6, 2-18
   precautionary with power, 3-2
   short field, 2-18
   without engine power, 3-2
Landing Gear Servicing, inside back cover
   main/nose wheel tire pressure, inside back cover
   nose gear shock strut servicing, inside back cover
Let-Down, 1-6
Lighting Equipment, 2-6
   exterior lighting, 2-6
   interior lighting, 2-7
Limitations, Airspeed, 4-3
Limitations, Engine Operation, 4-3
Loading Arrangements Diagram, 4-5
Loading Graph, 4-7
Loading Problem, Sample, 4-6
Long Range Fuel Tanks, 2-3
Low Oil Pressure, 3-8

M

MAA Plate/Finish Trim Plate, 5-4
Magneto Check, 2-12
Magneto Malfunction, 3-8
Maneuvers - Normal Category, 4-1
Maneuvers - Utility Category, 4-2
Markings, Airspeed Indicator, 4-3
Markings, Engine Instrument, 4-3
Master Switch, 2-4, 2-5
Maximum Glide Diagram, 6-6
Maximum Performance Take-Off, 1-5
Maximum Rate-Of-Climb Data Chart, 6-3
Microphone-Headset, 7-4

Moment Envelope, Center of
    Gravity, 4-8
Mooring Your Airplane, 5-1

N

Noise Abatement, 2-22
Normal Category Maneuvers, 4-1
Normal Landing, 1-6, 2-17
Normal Take-Off, 1-5
Nose Gear Shock Strut, inside back
    cover

O

Oil System,
    capacity, inside back cover
    oil/filter change, inside back
        cover
    oil grade, inside back cover
    pressure gage, 4-3
    quick-drain valve, 7-6
    temperature gage, 4-3
Operation, Cold Weather, 2-18
Operation, Hot Weather, 2-21
Operation Limitations, Engine, 4-3
Operations Authorized, 4-1
Over-Voltage Sensor and Warning
    Light, 2-5
Owner Follow-Up System, 5-8
    publications, 5-9

P

Painted Surfaces, 5-2
Performance - Specifications,
    inside front cover
Power Check, 2-13
Precautionary Landing with Engine
    Power, 3-2
Principal Dimensions Diagram, ii

Progressive Care, Cessna, 5-7
Propeller,
    care, 5-3
Publications, 5-9

Q

Quick Drain Valve, Oil, 7-6
Quick-Drain Valves, Fuel, 2-3

R

Radio Selector Switches, 7-3
    operation, 7-3
    speaker-phone switches, 7-4
    transmitter selector switch,
        7-3
Recovery From Spiral Dive, 3-6
Rough Engine Operation Or Loss of
    Power, 3-7
    carburetor icing, 3-7
    low oil pressure, 3-8
    magneto malfunction, 3-8
    spark plug fouling, 3-7

S

Sample Loading Problem, 4-6
Seat Belts and Shoulder Harnesses,
    2-9
Securing Aircraft, 1-7
Servicing Requirements, 5-8
    inside back cover
        engine oil, inside back cover
        fuel, inside back cover
        landing gear, inside back cover
Short Field Landing, 2-18
Shoulder Harnesses and Seat Belts,
    2-9
Spark Plug Fouling, 3-7
Speaker-Phone Switches, 7-4

Spins, 2-17
Stalls, 2-17
    speed chart, 6-2
Starting Engine, 1-4, 2-10
    cold weather, 2-18
Static Pressure Alternate Source Valve, 7-2
Storage, Flyable, 5-6
Surfaces,
    aluminum, 5-3
    painted, 5-2
System,
    cabin heating, ventilating and defrosting, 2-8
    electrical, 2-3
    fuel, 2-1
    owner follow-up, 5-8
    wing flap, 2-8

T

Table of Contents, iii
Tachometer, 4-4
Take-Off, 1-5, 2-13
    before, 1-4, 2-12
    crosswind, 2-14
    data chart, 6-3
    maximum performance, 1-5
    normal, 1-5
    performance charts, 2-14
    power check, 2-13
    wing flap settings, 2-14
Taxiing, 2-12
    diagram, 2-11
Tire Pressure, inside back cover
Transmitter Selector Switch, 7-3
True Airspeed Indicator, 7-5

U

Utility Category Maneuvers, 4-2

W

Warm-Up, 2-12
Weight,
    empty, inside front cover
    gross, inside front cover
Weight and Balance, 4-4
    center of gravity moment envelope, 4-8
    loading arrangements diagram, 4-5
    loading graph, 4-7
    sample loading problem, 4-6
Windshield - Windows, 5-2
Wing Flap Settings, Take-Off, 2-14
Wing Flap System, 2-8
Winterization Kit, 7-1

SERVICING REQUIREMENTS *

ENGINE OIL:

GRADE -- Aviation Grade SAE 50 Above 60°F.
  Aviation Grade SAE 10W30 or SAE 30 Between 0° and 70°F.
  Aviation Grade SAE 10W30 or SAE 20 Below 10°F.
Multi-viscosity oil with a range of SAE 10W30 is recommended for improved starting in cold weather. Detergent or dispersant oil, conforming to Specification No. MIL-L-22851, must be used.

NOTE

Your Cessna was delivered from the factory with a corrosion preventive aircraft engine oil If oil must be added during the first 25 hours, use only aviation grade straight mineral oil (non-detergent) conforming to Specification No. MIL-L-6082.

CAPACITY OF ENGINE SUMP -- 8 Quarts.
  Do not operate on less than 6 quarts. To minimize loss of oil through breather, fill to 7 quart level for normal flights of less than 3 hours. For extended flight, fill to 8 quarts. These quantities refer to oil dipstick level readings. During oil and oil filter changes, one additional quart is required when the filter element is changed.

OIL AND OIL FILTER CHANGE---
  After the first 25 hours of operation, drain engine oil sump and oil cooler and clean both the oil suction strainer and the oil pressure screen. If an optional oil filter is installed, change filter element at this time. Refill sump with straight mineral oil (non-detergent) and use until a total of 50 hours has accumulated or oil consumption has stabilized; then change to detergent oil. On aircraft not equipped with an optional oil filter, drain the engine oil sump and oil cooler and clean both the oil suction strainer and the oil pressure screen each 50 hours thereafter. On aircraft which have an optional oil filter, the oil change interval may be extended to 100-hour intervals, providing the oil filter element is changed at 50-hour intervals. Change engine oil at least every 6 months even though less than the recommended hours have accumulated. Reduce intervals for prolonged operation in dusty areas, cold climates, or when short flights and long idle periods result in sludging conditions.

SERVICING REQUIREMENTS*

FUEL:

GRADE -- 80/87 Minimum Grade Aviation Fuel.
  Alternate fuels which are also approved are:
  100/130 Low Lead AVGAS (maximum lead content of 2 c.c. per gallon)
  100/130 Aviation Grade Fuel (maximum lead content of 4.6 c.c. per gallon)

NOTE

When substituting a higher octane fuel, low lead AVGAS 100 should be used whenever possible since it will result in less lead contamination of the engine.

CAPACITY EACH STANDARD TANK -- 21 Gallons.
CAPACITY EACH LONG RANGE TANK -- 26 Gallons.

NOTE

To ensure maximum fuel capacity when refueling, place the fuel selector valve in either LEFT or RIGHT position to prevent cross-feeding.

LANDING GEAR:

NOSE WHEEL TIRE PRESSURE -- 31 PSI on 5.00-5, 4-Ply Rated Tire.
                           26 PSI on 6.00-6, 4-Ply Rated Tire.
MAIN WHEEL TIRE PRESSURE -- 29 PSI on 6.00-6, 4-Ply Rated Tires.
NOSE GEAR SHOCK STRUT --
  Keep filled with MIL-H-5606 hydraulic fluid and inflated with air to 45 PSI.

*For complete servicing requirements, refer to the aircraft Service Manual.

www.ingramcontent.com/pod-product-compliance
Lightning Source LLC
LaVergne TN
LVHW060142080526
838202LV00049B/4056